UCA

university for the **creative arts**

Farnham
Falkner Road
Farnham
Surrey
GU9 7DS

Tel: 01252 892709
Fax: 01252 892725
e-mail: libraryfarn@ucreative.ac.uk

editing & post-production

screencraft

declan mcgrath

editing & post-production

screencraft

RotoVision

A RotoVision Book

Published and distributed by RotoVision SA

Rue du Bugnon 7

CH-1299 Crans-Près-Céligny

Switzerland

RotoVision SA, Sales & Production Office

Sheridan House, 112/116A Western Road

Hove, East Sussex BN3 1DD, UK

Tel: +44 (0)1273 727 268

Fax: +44 (0)1273 727 269

E-mail: sales@rotovision.com

Website: www.rotovision.com

ISBN 2-88046-555-9

10 9 8 7 6 5 4 3 2 1

Design Copyright © 1998 Morla Design, Inc., San Francisco

Layout by Artmedia, London

Production and separation by ProVision Pte. Ltd., Singapore

Tel: +65 334 7720

Fax: +65 334 7721

contents

introduction

This book is about what happens in post-production – the period after a film has been shot. The actual shooting of a movie may only take eight weeks, but it could easily be another eight months before the post-production is complete. What happens during those months is a mystery to many, including most of the shooting crew. Everything they shot was meticulously planned with the final film in mind, so why do they have to wait up to a year to see the results of their work? Is it not simply a case of picking the best material, joining up the shots and adding some music? In the pages that follow, 15 of the world's top editors reveal what exactly does happen during the months of post-production. By sharing the secrets of their trade, they tell us how films are really put together.

Not all the editors approached wanted to take part in this book. After much deliberation one world-class editor felt that by talking about their work they risked destroying the magic of film – leaving for the audience the mere mechanical flashing every second of 24 frames of picture and sound on to a white screen. It was a risk they were not prepared to take.

Having read this book perhaps you will notice every cut or visual effect next time you are at the cinema. After reading the interview with Skip Lievsay, sound editor of **The Silence of the Lambs** and **GoodFellas**, you may even hear the foley and ADR, and become aware of every sound effect. Be warned! This could seriously hamper your enjoyment. Perhaps consider the opinion of Mark Berger who was the re-recording mixer on **Apocalypse Now**. He believes that learning about the techniques of post-production is similar to learning about the techniques of classical music. When you learn at first about a Mozart symphony or a Bach cantata, you will be distracted. You will notice each of the instruments. You will become aware of the construction and rhythms of the piece. Eventually, however, you will return to hearing the whole symphony or cantata as one piece. Your enjoyment will be as before, but your appreciation will be all the greater. Similarly, being aware of the individual cuts and sounds that make up a film can enrich your overall experience as a viewer. That awareness would never prevent a good film from casting its spell, because in a good film the story and characters become real and the mechanics no longer matter.

The contributions that follow will not only let you in on the secrets of the cutting room, but they also make up an alternative history of cinema. Every craft or department in feature film-making will argue its central importance to the making of a film. That is the way it should be. Such pride and self-belief makes the contribution of a camera operator, production designer or any other film craftsman great. But while every craft is essential to the making of a film, editing, unlike photography or sound recording, has the distinction of being unique to the making of films. When cinema was invented, at the start of the last century, there were already writers, actors, musicians, photographers and set-designers. There was no such thing as a film editor. Editing grew along with cinema as part of a new cinematic language which manipulated time and controlled the viewpoint of the audience.

The very first films contained no cuts. They consisted of just one continuous shot. The Lumière Brothers' **Arrival of a Train** (1895), for example, shows a train arriving at a station – in one shot with no cuts. Other films showed dramas being acted out, similarly in one continuous wide shot without a single edit. Once film-makers realised that you could actually

"cut" these shots together it allowed them to create longer films of similar single shots assembled in story order. This was the earliest editing.

A huge step was the discovery that the film-maker could cut away from one scene in one location to a completely different scene in another location and that the viewer would accept it. You can show a girl under attack in her home and then cut to a shot of the hero riding to her rescue. Somehow the audience realises that the two events are happening simultaneously and that the hero is going to the girl. Keep cutting between the threatened girl and the rescuing hero and you build up tension and excitement. The story and the drama are created in the cutting room. The new language of cinema develops.

Next it was discovered that the way we perceive reality could be totally changed in the cutting room, when film-makers actually dared to cut within a scene. Start with a wide shot showing two characters and suddenly cut into a close-up showing just one character. Nowadays we accept our point of view being constantly moved around every time we go to the cinema or watch TV, but in the early days of cinema the studios felt that cutting within a scene was too radical, and that it would disturb the audience. As Walter Murch, editor of **The Godfather** and **Apocalypse Now**, points out, nothing in the previous history of the human race prepared us for the visual shift in point of view that happens every time the editor makes a cut. It is hard to imagine now, but it would not have been surprising if people had never accepted these dramatic jumps in time and space. All the pioneers of editing featured here agree on one thing: that the innovations made in the cutting room – from the slow pace of cutting in the early talkies to the frenetic MTV style often seen today – are only made with the collusion of the film-going audience. It only works when the audience accepts it.

The development of editing (and thus cinema) began in the silent cutting rooms. It is there that Ralph Winters, editor of **High Society** and **The Thomas Crown Affair**, began to learn his trade. Ralph notes that the style accepted by movie audiences in the 1940s differed significantly from what audiences expected when television arrived in the 1950s. In the 1940s there was often little cutting within scenes and few close-ups. There was also more emphasis placed on the director using composition within the frame rather than cutting to tell the story. When Anne Coates began to edit in the 1950s, an editor could not cut directly from one time or place to another – you had to fade out and fade in. By the 1960s, Cécile Decugis, editor of many French New Wave films, was cutting shots together in a manner that made them seem to jump rather than smoothly flow. At the time this was revolutionary, but now the "jump-cut" is accepted. Such techniques are being pushed further today with Jill Bilcock's quick editing on **William Shakespeare's Romeo & Juliet** and the stylistic jump-cutting of William Chang, editor of **Happy Together** and **In the Mood for Love**. The language of cinema has been changing and what people accept has altered. The cockpit of this change has been the cutting room. Pietro Scalia's approach to **Gladiator** in 2000, with his access to computer-generated imagery and sophisticated sound effects, was completely different to Ralph Winters' approach to **Ben-Hur** in 1959. Of course flashy editing effects do not make good editing, indeed it is more likely that they make bad editing. As Jim Clark stridently declares, the best editing is the editing you don't see.

Whatever the style, the cutting room should be (to quote Yoshinori Ota) like a laboratory. It is a place where the editor constantly experiments, trying to find the way of putting together the finest bits of all of the available shots in the arrangement that best suits the picture. This process is the third and final rewrite of the film coming after the writing of the script and the changes made while shooting. Jacques Witta tells us that the editor is searching to find the magic that is contained somewhere on those bits of plastic that make up the film. In the course of this book, you will hopefully get a glimpse of how that magic is discovered.

What follows is an insider's account of what goes on in the cutting room. It is told by some of the world's top editors – those who fashioned the material of many of the best films of the last century. As well as covering the history of cinema, these editors – coming from China, Italy, the UK, France, Japan, Australia and the US – illustrate the international nature of this 20th-century craft and art form. Together they offer the reader samples of different styles and approaches to their craft. Their story is rarely heard, because few understand the importance of the editors' job. It is also rarely told because editors are generally a humble self-effacing lot – a characteristic that suits the collaborative nature of the job and the close-knit politics of the cutting room. In this book you can read Dede Allen's interview where she explains how editors work with actors long after those actors have left the film by moulding their performances in the cutting room. Paul Hirsch reveals how the editor moves the audience to the edge of their seats by putting together the footage in a way that builds up drama and tension.

It is an opportune time for such a book. The recent replacement of 35mm film print in the cutting room by digital technology has changed the craft and work methods practised there. For almost 100 years editors physically cut the film and taped it together. This manual process was labour-intensive and required a team of assistants. Increasingly editors now cut in the virtual environment of a computer, using fewer assistants. The editors featured in this book are at different stages of this changeover, but soon they will all work on computers. The artistry that makes an editor good will be the same, but the film craft will be lost and there will no longer be assistants learning their craft from those who went before. As well as being revolutionised, the crafts of post-production will be democratised. Anyone with a home computer will have access to more or less the same technology as the editor of a big-budget feature. The future will reveal whether more editors means better editors, but remember that more artists now graduate from art college each year than ever lived in Renaissance Italy. As in the film cutting rooms, during Renaissance times the production of a painting involved a whole team of apprentices and assistants who spent years learning their craft.

My own experience of the cutting rooms began as a young teenager when my Uncle Jim McGrath bought me a roll of film for my father's Super 8mm camera. I shot a film (starring Frank, Rosemary and Nuala McGrath) based on the adventures of a comic book hero. When the film arrived back there was, however, no way to view it. So I cut out each of the shots and hung all of them up on a piece of string using clothes pegs. I stuck the film together as best I could without any projection facilities and entered it into a competition for young film-makers. The film arrived back with an accompanying note applauding my efforts, but with the suggestion that more time should have been spent in the editing. Not only was the story confusing in parts, but some of the shots were upside-down! Yoshinori Ota may use clothes pegs to hang his trims, but apart from that there is no comparison between my efforts and the artistry of those who follow. Since then my own knowledge and skill in editing has hopefully developed having worked as an apprentice, assistant and editor. At least I learnt the value of viewing what you edit. But it was with the awe and excitement of that 13-year-old that I met the masters who feature in this book. I would like to thank each of them for the generosity with which they received me.

To Natalia Price-Cabrera, Editor-in-Chief at RotoVision, goes my primary thanks and appreciation for allowing me the opportunity to put this book together and to meet my wish-list of editing heroes. Her patience, support and good humour made writing it both possible and pleasurable. Credit goes to the rest of the team at RotoVision including Laura Owen and Nicole Mendelsohn. Andrea Bettella and Francesca Wisniewska at Artmedia deserve the utmost praise for the excellent design work. Judith Burns painstakingly typed up the transcripts of all the interviews and was always accommodating. I am also grateful to Claudine Favrat (who facilitated the interviews with Jacques Witta and Cécile Decugis), Makoto Kakurai (who facilitated the interview with Yoshinori Ota) and Charlotte Yu (who facilitated the interview with William Chang). Lisa Dosch of ACE was very helpful in tracking down contributors in the US. Many fine editors, although they did not take part, supported this project. I must particularly thank Dermot Diskin, Mary Finlay, George Akers, Anna Maria O'Flanagan, Michael Doyle, Anthony Litton, Claire Kilroy, Niamh Fagan, Emer Reynolds, Allen Zaleski, Doug Murray, Se Merry Doyle, Anne O'Leary and Ardmore Sound. Thanks also to good friends and film-makers Bruce Naughton and Robert Taylor for their helpful nagging! Also to Sean O'Neill in Leitrim and Aisling O'Leary in Cork for providing shelter from the storm of Dublin when required. Special thanks to Felim Mac Dermott, who not only worked on this book as photographer and researcher, but without whose encouragement and support it would simply never have happened. Finally, I would like to dedicate this book to Rosemary McGrath and the memory of Frank McGrath. Go raibh mile maith agaibh.

DECLAN MCGRATH

Born in Toronto, Canada, Ralph Winters started working in the cutting rooms with MGM in 1928 at the age of 18. "I could not afford to go to college and felt that I would not get the best out of studying if I had to work my way through, so I decided to go and work in the cutting rooms. My Father, who was a tailor with MGM, knew the head of the cutting department and so he gave me an introduction." Ralph

ralph winters

worked his way up through the ranks, learning his craft by assisting older and more experienced editors. He got his break when he was working in the shorts department at MGM. "I was editing a four-reel short. When we got it all finished the company discovered there was no release for it." At that time they had releases for two-reelers, but not four-reelers. "So they decided to elaborate on it and make it a feature length movie. They wrote some stuff and it became a seven-reeler. That was my first feature credit." Ralph went on to edit 75 feature films. He has been nominated for six Academy Awards for best editing on **Kotch** (1971, Jack Lemmon), **The Great Race** (1965, Blake Edwards), **Ben-Hur** (1959, William Wyler and Andrew Marton), **Seven Brides for Seven Brothers** (1954, Stanley Donen), **Quo Vadis?** (1951, Mervyn LeRoy), and **King Solomon's Mines** (1950, Compton Bennett), winning the Oscar twice with **Ben-Hur** and **King Solomon's Mines**.

The job of an editor is to make a picture as good as it can possibly be. I do not think that the general public should be too aware of the editing process. When someone goes to a film they should be able to sit down and watch it without being conscious of the cutting. I started as an assistant editor at MGM in the silent days. Everything, compared with the way it is today, was extremely primitive, but the studios were good places to work. In the old days the people were very nice and it was like a family. The studio heads like Carl Mayer and Louis Laemmle grew up with the film. They loved film. Today they love money. MGM was making a picture a week in those days and they had about 35 editors. Each studio had their own group of people working for them. MGM had tremendous quality, they had the money and the wherewithal to accumulate the right kind of people and people at MGM never had any trouble getting jobs anywhere. In the early, early days editors were not even given positive prints so that they could cut and experiment. Pictures were shot and the negative was cut and then the release prints were made. So there was no real cutting as such. As things got better and bigger, editors were able to work on a positive to get the best cut and they were called cutters. It has changed today because editors now work on computers, which enable them to do things a lot quicker, and I think in many ways, a lot better. These machines give you a lot of leeway because you can store a lot of different versions of a cut. I think editors are very highly regarded today and they do make a tremendous contribution. However, because the cutting is done on computer, directors and producers now think that they can do the editing themselves. It always fascinated me that no producer or director ever thought that he could photograph a picture or that he could be the production designer – or anything else on the picture – but somehow most producers and directors think they can edit. Unfortunately they cannot. A lot of them do not understand it. They cannot recognise good editing and they accept less than the best because they do not know what the best is.

Ben-Hur was certainly regarded as a huge film at the time. It had a budget of $12 million. Billy Wyler printed about 600,000 feet and I think he exposed about a million and a quarter feet of negative to get that. So we had 600,000 feet to work with in the cutting room and each one of those feet contained 16 frames of film, so we would have had 9,600,600 frames to choose from in the cutting room! The chariot race alone had about 60,000 feet printed! So it was certainly intimidating to start cutting it. They could not shoot the whole race all in one day, so I did not get all the film in one day.

There were eight laps, but they were not shot in continuity. So you might be editing the material for the seventh or the fifth lap and then the fourth lap. You were jumping around all the time between laps until you got the whole race together. To know where I was, I had a big chart on the wall with the laps of the race and I entered the shots on it as I got them. Then I had to put my head down and start to put it together. Then I would take a look and see how it worked, slowly pulling it together, kneading it and working it.

An action sequence like the chariot race is something that you just have to cut and re-cut and keep changing since it does not have the scripted continuity of a dialogue scene. The first cut would have been quite rough – about 1,100 feet. That cut had all the necessary elements, but it did not have any of the pace or tempo. Then we pared it down, making the cuts shorter and building up the rhythm. At first, most of the material was shot with doubles, but when they found out that both Chuck Heston and Steve Boyd could drive the chariots themselves they redid a lot of the medium shots and close-ups using the two of them. Once this had been shot I went through the footage and started pruning out the material with doubles and replaced it with the new material featuring the actual actors. That made it a lot better, a lot more real. There are no rules for action sequences – it just depends on how it's shot and the type of material you get. You have to put it together some way to begin with and then you work it down very slowly and carefully. You save all the good pieces. The best and safest place for a good piece of film is right in the cut sequence itself until you are sure that you need to remove it

1   2

3

4

(1–4) Before the advent of television in the late 1950s, films were often characterised by less cutting and a greater use of wide shots. For example, in **High Society** a lot of the shots were played out with little cutting. "The director, Chuck Walters, was originally a choreographer and a stage director and he saw everything from the viewpoint of the stage. He did not know enough about the cinematic medium to use shots as well as he could have, but he still was a hell of a good director. If he shot a scene with two good actors, and if the scene played well and felt good to him, he saw no need to shoot close-ups. He was used to that kind of thinking from the stage."

(1–4) "The numbers in these two movies were not designed for a lot of quick cutting. Anyway, in dance numbers an audience should see as much as possible of the full figure at all times. Hence less cutting if the shot holds up. I do not think cutting and shooting these same numbers today would change much. Again, such things are up to the director's style. On **Seven Brides for Seven Brothers** (1–3) they laid out every musical shot very carefully, they just overlapped a little bit and they had a place where they wanted to cut. All of the musical sequences you might say were camera-cut. I loved working on that picture. This sequence shows one musical number called Lonesome Polecat lasting three and a half minutes which was played out in one shot with no cuts. The musical number called Main Street from **On the Town** (4) contained four shots and only three cuts."

4

5

6

"The coming of sound was very scary to everyone. It was mysterious and foreboding. The atmosphere in the cutting room did change. Dramatically. No more tearing of film at the point of cut. Neat work with scissors had to be applied. Now editors cut on computers. Technology may change, but a good editor has to know his story well and know how to dramatise it. Editorial skill takes precedent over mechanics every time." Scenes in the cutting room (5–6).

"Billy Wilder (4) hated close-ups. His staging was absolutely wonderful and he always had the actors in front of the camera at the important part of the scene. Therefore if he did not have close-ups you never really did feel that you needed them. He had staged the shot so that the audience saw what they had to see without you having to cut to close-ups. I think that was terrific, and very few directors can do that. I remember one time on **The Front Page** (1–5) he said to me: 'I have to apologise to you today Ralph, I shot close-ups.' But when I saw the film I said to him: 'Don't worry about that, I can always use them.' They were not really close-ups. They were sort of close shots! Billy was and is a brilliant guy."

for some reason. An action scene needs to be made dramatic through the actors. The chariot race in **Ben-Hur** could be quite bland since essentially it is merely a load of chariots racing round a track. What makes it dramatic is the conflict between two people – two men that we know were once great friends and who have now become great enemies. Then we cut to the sheikh in the stands who acts as a counterpoint to the drama on the track. I worked on that sequence for three solid months. During that time, I never touched another piece of film. So the amount of film on the rest of the picture just grew, getting bigger and tougher. However, we had to get the chariot race finished since there was such a big overhead in Rome. There were four horses for each of the nine teams in the race; that's 36 horses. Each team had doubles, that's 72 horses, then all the ponies and the cowboys that had to ride them. So we had a veritable stable on the back lot of Cinnecittà in Rome! The production company obviously wanted to get through the sequence as quickly as possible so that they could dismiss the company (which happened long before the entire picture was finished).

I came from a school of editing where, when a director shot a scene which held up and it played well enough so that the audience could watch two or three people without any inter-cutting, we would keep that shot and let it run. We let the audiences eyes go where they wanted them to go. We allowed people to relate to the character they wanted to without cutting to close-ups. I always felt that was a wonderful way to show a story. The audience can shift their eyes to what they want to see instead of being directed by the editor cutting in close-ups. What directors should worry about today is working on a scene and getting the right performances, never mind how they are going to cut it. Of course when television came along you had to cut because the screen was so small. You had to cut to faces for the audience to see expressions. I think audiences got used to that and it crept into the editing of feature pictures too. If you do not go clumsily from one close-up to another or clumsily from medium shots to close-ups, but rather if you are doing it rhythmically and for a reason, then I do not think any kind of cutting will disturb an audience.

Nowadays they do a lot of things we would not have thought of doing in the old days, but they get away with it. I think that this is due to television. When you look at enough television you begin to accept certain things like quick cutting and other types of cutting which are not well executed in the classical sense. Audiences' eyes today are quicker, they can see things better and you have to be aware of this when you cut. I recently watched an old movie and they played this long scene with two people sitting on the front steps of a home. There was no cutting in it yet it was a wonderful thing to watch since it just had a flow to it. I think a lot of the directors today are just not capable of getting that kind of a scene or maybe the actors aren't capable of delivering it. But I rarely see a scene that is uncut today. That is the way they shoot it nowadays. They shoot so much film and then they throw it into the cutting room and they expect the editor to do something with it, which of course he does at times.

When an editor has a tremendous amount of film to cut, there

1

3

4

(5) "An action scene needs to be made dramatic through the actors. The chariot race in **Ben-Hur** could be quite bland – effectively it is just a load of chariots racing round a track. What makes it dramatic is the conflict between two people – two men that we know were once great friends and who have now become great enemies. Then we cut to the sheikh in the stands who acts as a counterpoint to the drama on the track."

2

5

6

(1–5) "I worked on the chariot race in black and white too because they did not want to print the colour until the sequence was cut and that was tough. I had to memorise the look of it because I did not have the advantage of the colourful costumes to keep the teams separated. This sequence was kind of like a nightmare! The director of **Ben-Hur**, William Wyler (6), was a brilliant man, but he was irritable – he was deaf in one ear and I think that created his irritable feeling all the time. He was tough to work for. He was a no-nonsense fellow, but he did such great work you just had to admire the way he shot stuff. It was something to work for him."

1

"The chess sequence was the only sequence I put together on **The Thomas Crown Affair** (1–2) and then they gave me a credit on it. I did not think that I had deserved a credit and did not want it, but they insisted that I have it. It was a tough sequence; all nuances and innuendo. There were some very interesting pieces of film in the dailies – but no planned continuity. I spent a day or two studying the film before I cut anything. It is by inter-cutting a shot of a chess piece with a close-up of the hands of the actors that you begin to get into the sequence, creating the kind of thinking that you want the audience to have. It was a very sexy, suggestive sequence."

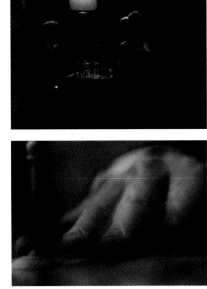

2

are all kinds of ways to approach a sequence because he has all kinds of angles, long shots, medium shots and close-ups to choose from. For example, in a sequence like the chess sequence in **The Thomas Crown Affair** (1968, Norman Jewison) you could open on anything. As with an action sequence, it does not have that kind of continuity you have with a dialogue sequence. Even when a dialogue scene is complicated, you have at least a pattern, which the words follow as laid out in the script. Something like the chess sequence is tough, but whenever I had anything like this I would start in a very orthodox way. I open on a long shot so that we know where we are and then I play that long shot for whatever I think it's worth. Then I cut to this close-up and then I cut to that close-up. The quickest way to get into trouble when you are editing a sequence is to start to get fancy right away and open up on some close-up and then you cut to this and you cut to that, because you are trying to show the director some clever and brilliant way of doing it that he never thought about. That is the quickest way to get into trouble. I always kept everything as orthodox as I could. Only when I got it together would I look at it and say: "I'm not going to open on that long shot, here's that piece of film, that's going to work, I'm going to open up on that." I would try then that new way. Maybe it would not work just because I thought it would. So I would go back and do it again. I would try it again and again and again. Never think that when you see something on the screen that that is the way it was done the first time. Maybe once in every four or five pictures I cut a sequence that I did not have to touch again. That was a reason to go out and get drunk that night because you happened to be

lucky enough to hit it! You have to work things up and that is the way the chariot race was done. Good editing comes from long, hard, grinding work. There are no miracles in the cutting room – you make what you can out of the material that you have been handed. Sometimes I have worked and worked on a sequence and I still cannot make it look good because the material just is not there. But at the end of the day you make it as good as it can be – that is your job.

biography

Yoshinori Ota was born in Yokohama, Japan in 1961. He went to film school at Yokohama Housou Eiga Senmon Gakuin (Yokohama Academy of Television and Film). There he became drawn to editing. Before film school he had thought that when you watched a film you were watching it the way that it always had to be. It was through the editing classes at film school that he learnt that there is not just one story in a

yoshinori ota

film, rather there are infinite possibilities of stories and it is the editor who controls those possibilities. After college he started out as an assistant editor on television dramas and documentaries. Eventually he became editor of direct-to-video dramas before moving on to feature films. His first collaboration with Takeshi Kitano was as a consultant on his third feature, **A Scene at the Sea** (1991). This film was Kitano's first on which he worked as an editor. Yoshinori has worked on all Kitano's films since, including **Sonatine** (1993), **Hana-Bi** (1997), **Kikujiro** (1999) and **Brother** (2000). "At first, I thought Mr Kitano would become bored of the editing process, however, film by film, his knowledge and artistic talent toward editing deepened and he is now able to work around conventional editing, exploring and experimenting freely. I am there to support him and make suggestions."

interview

For me editing equals experimenting. Around the world editors are the first to see the shots from any film. They are then the first to put these shots together, trying out ideas and beginning to work the material. Sometimes their results are a success, other times not, but this is the process which makes editing an experiment. All my own editing is done on film. This is how movies have been cut since the invention of cinema. However, in the last few years in many countries editors have started cutting on computers. I suppose this is like moving from an old typewriter to a word processor with fancy desktop publishing capabilities. It is quite a revolutionary change. During the shooting of **Brother** I had the opportunity to visit Los Angeles. I was amazed at the advanced environment of post-production facilities there. Most people in LA are now working on computer non-linear systems. In Japan there is only one film studio that has such a system. The equipment we are using has not changed since the 1960s. Indeed the basic system has changed little since

(1–19) **Hana-Bi:** During the killing at a kiosk in **Hana-Bi** the soundtrack goes to silence (1–12). "The emphasis here is not the depiction of the killing itself, but on the emotions of Nishi who is looking on at the incident." Flashbacks in **Hana-Bi** are often played in slow-motion to similarly "emphasise the emotional impact of the incident on Nishi. The style of **Hana-Bi** was not to emphasise the words or actions of each character. Rather the most important consideration was how to evoke strong emotions from just silence."

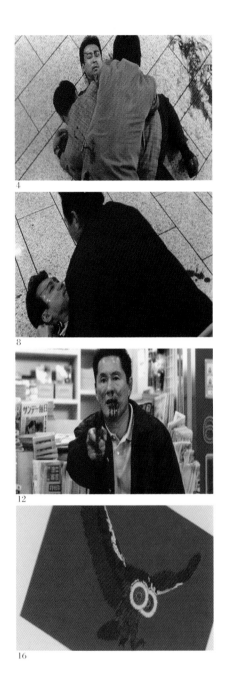

4

8

12

16

17

18

19

Throughout **Hana-Bi** stills of paintings are inter-cut with the action (13–16). "The effect was, through the paintings, to let the audience feel each of the character's emotions and agony. From the beginning Mr Kitano had an idea to use these paintings, but no definite vision of how. By experimenting on a daily basis in the cutting room he found a way of using them."

27

yoshinori ota

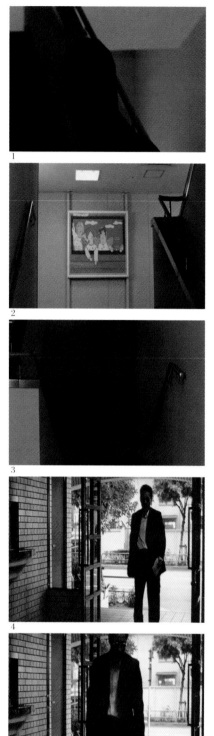

In **Hana-Bi** (1–10) characters walk out of a frame and the empty frame is held before cutting to the next shot. The Hollywood editor would rarely allow such "empty space" to remain on screen. For Yoshinori, "this effect leaves the emotion of the character or characters on screen."

the beginning of cinema. I wish that the Japanese film industry would make efforts to improve the editing and post-production facilities, however, I would never suggest that the improvement of facilities is an important factor in editing. Essentially good editing comes from the editor's craft and technical skill. Pieces of equipment are just tools. I understand from my stay in Los Angeles that this basic mentality is the same in the USA. In my view, cutting on film is the easiest and clearest way of editing. One of the advantages of this method is that when you screen film you can see the colours and contrast of the picture. This is extremely important. That is why all of Kitano's pictures are edited on film and not on computer. He is famous for his "Kitano Blue" and if you cut on computer you cannot avoid all the colours and contrast taking on a video texture.

The advantage of working on computer is that it allows the editor instant access to each of the shots which have been digitised into the computer. On computer the editor can make changes quickly and constantly change the cut without actually touching the film (just as a writer can do with a word processor). In a film cutting room you are physically cutting frames of film and sticking them back together with Sellotape. Because it takes more time to do things on film the rhythm of work is more relaxed. The director and editor are not presented with many options at one time – it takes time just to make one cut on film so this gives the director more time to think. On computer the thought process is rushed as everything can be done so quickly. Running a film cutting room involves a lot of work to keep the film in good condition

and make it constantly accessible to the editor. Essentially the assistant must be able to locate every single frame of picture and its matching frame of sound quickly and efficiently to allow me to edit the film. This is quite an achievement when you consider that the average film is around 110 minutes. That makes it 10,000 feet long. Every foot contains 16 frames of picture. So the average film contains 160,000 frames of picture and 160,000 matching frames of sound! Then consider the fact that you may have shot five times that amount to pick from. (That is a conservative estimate, particularly for bigger budget movies.) That would mean that in an average cutting room you must be able to locate any one of 800,000 frames of picture and match it to the corresponding frame of sound (of which there are also 800,000).

The process starts with my assistant receiving both the picture and sound on separate pieces of film in the cutting room the day after they have been shot. The assistant will sync up each bit of picture with the correct piece of sound. Every shot must be marked with a pencil or marker according to the shot number and scene to identify it. These numbers allow us to match the correct piece of sound to the correct piece of film. For example, 74–1–2 means that the piece of film is from scene 74, slate (or set-up) 1, take 2. There are other parts of the system and pieces of paperwork which allow the assistant to quickly locate the required piece of sound or picture while keeping track of everything in the film, including all the extra sound and picture effects that get added to the film during post-production. Once the daily

Movies are still basically cut on film in Japan. In other countries the editor may cut on computer while a team of assistants simultaneously match the cut on film which can be used for screenings. Thus, if the budget allows, the editor still has the advantages of screening on film. However, there will be a time lapse before the assistants have "conformed" the print to the computer cut. Yoshinori views the film on his upright editing machine (1). The picture and sound are separately fed in from a horse (2) and go through the viewer on to a synchroniser (3) which keeps picture and sound in sync. From the synchroniser the film spools into cotton bins. Yoshinori controls what he sees on the viewer with two pedals under the table (4). One is for forward motion, the other for backwards. He can mark where he wants to cut with a Chinagraph pencil (5). He or an assistant will then cut the film with a splicer (6). Joins are made with Sellotape on the same splicer (7). He or an assistant will engrave a number on the side of the film he has cut (8). This means it can be properly filed and found again. All the trims created by the cutting are handed to an assistant who will sort them out in a neighbouring bin – hanging them with clothes pegs (9). All of the film will be stored in carefully marked rolls (13) so that the assistant can easily access any piece of film the editor needs. Running a film cutting room requires much organisation with its trims, filing systems and mechanical numbering to identify every frame of film. Paperwork referred to when managing a film in the cutting room (10–12, 19–21).

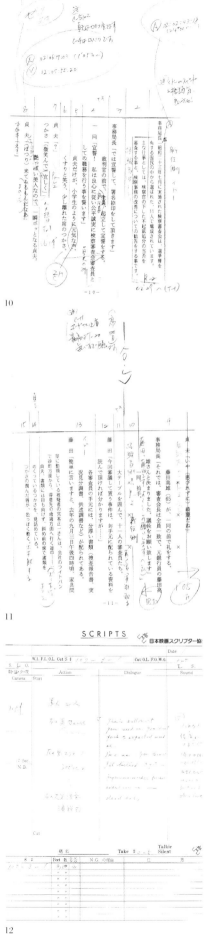

10

11

12

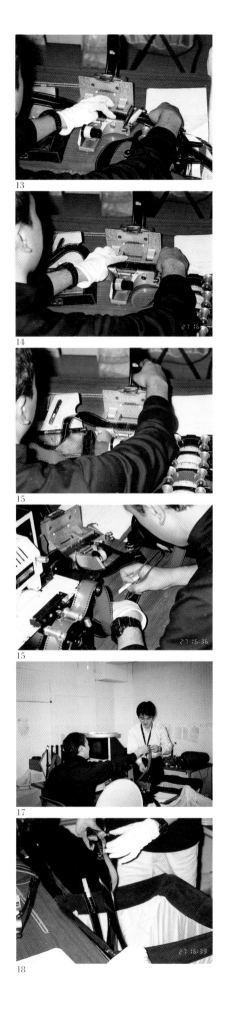

13

14

15

16

17

18

SCRIPTS 日本映画スクリプター協

19

20

21

1

2

3

4

5

6

7

8

9

10

11

12

13

14

15

(2) Akira Kurosawa's dynamic editing of **Seven Samurai** (1, 3–8) had a huge influence on international cinema as well as the young Yoshinori Ota: "Some of Kurosawa's editing is actually not good in technical or continuity terms, but there is a dynamism that works in his films as a whole. He taught me that it is not enough for an editor to just be technical, you must also be dynamic!" The carefully composed still frames (the camera does not move) in **Kikujiro** (9–14) echo the style of Japanese film-maker Yasujiro Ozu (15), particularly on **Tokyo Story**. But for Yoshinori "I do not believe that Mr Kitano is obsessed with still frames. I believe he just does not move the camera because he sees no reason to do so!"

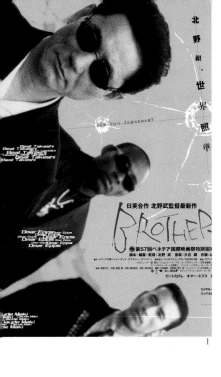

editing & post-production

"During the shooting of **Brother** (1–4) I had the opportunity to visit Los Angeles. I was amazed at the advanced environment of post-production facilities there. Most people in LA are now working on computer non-linear systems. In Japan there is only one film studio that has such a system."

rushes have been prepared by my assistants they will be screened that evening for the director and crew. This allows the crew to check what they have shot. We make sure that there are no scratches, the colour is good and the lighting and sound have worked. When I start cutting this material together I will look again at each and every take, both the okay and no-good shots, and I will memorise each one of them until I can remember every detail of every take. Once the shots have been memorised in this way I will be able to assemble them together in any way at any time upon the director's request. Only then do I begin cutting the footage together, trying to balance every cut with the entire film in mind.

Cutting during the shoot means I am able to screen sequences that have been actually cut together along with the daily rushes screenings. These daily screenings are important because they allow Mr Kitano and the entire crew to determine what needs to be shot next. While we are cutting we discover things never anticipated in the script. This is especially valuable during the shoot and is the reason why the script often gets constantly revised. It is Mr Kitano's style to shoot and edit at the same time. This means that there is a lot of going back and forth between the crew and the cutting room throughout the shoot with us letting the crew know what we need. Working this way with such regular screenings is a constant challenge to the crew. It makes them think, "What did we shoot today? Where are we today? What should we shoot tomorrow?" This is why I feel that such screenings are important. It is always the best way to judge what you have

cut together. Watching bright colours in a large dark room surrounded by theatrical sound will provoke the director's imagination as well as being the best environment for the crew to check their respective work. In the weeks after the shoot, when we have started cutting, Kitano will have the film projected every night after editing. He always says, "I want to see it a hundred times!" Of course producers will also want to view screenings throughout the editing process. I believe they have a lot of control in post-production. It is not that they spend time in the cutting room but once they make a point it is like a nuclear missile. Their influence is powerful. As the post-production process progresses the editor must also imagine what the final sound will be like. I will begin to think about the music and sound effects and how they will work with the pictures. There are no sound editors in Japan in the way that there are in the USA. In Japan it is usually the assistant editor who will do this job. In Japan sound editing experience is one of the steps to becoming an editor. It seems that post-production in the USA will continue to develop. I am sure that Japan and the rest of the world will move away from the old craft of the film cutting rooms towards a system based on digital computers. I hear that George Lucas is pursuing the possibility of transmitting digital film data and projecting it in theatres without using print. It would be wonderful if digital data could be the same quality as film in the future. Once that happens there will probably be no film in any stage of the film-making process. Many of the skills and crafts associated with the cutting rooms will disappear. But at the end of the day, for an editor, it just comes down to the same questions as always of where and what you cut.

biography

Walter Murch has been honoured by both British and American Motion Picture Academies for his picture editing and sound mixing. In 1997, Murch received an unprecedented double Oscar for both film editing and sound mixing on **The English Patient** (1996, Anthony Minghella), as well as the British Academy Award for best editing. 17 years earlier, he received an Oscar for best sound

walter murch

for **Apocalypse Now** (1979, Francis Ford Coppola), as well as British and American Academy nominations for his picture editing on the same film. Among his other credits are both picture editing and sound mixing on **The Conversation** (1974, Francis Ford Coppola), and picture editing on **Julia** (1977, Fred Zinnemann), **The Unbearable Lightness of Being** (1987, Philip Kaufman) and **The Talented Mr Ripley** (1999, Anthony Minghella). In 1998 he was responsible for a re-edit of **Touch of Evil** (1958, Orson Welles) based on instructions written by Welles. Murch was also the re-recording mixer for **The Rain People** (1969, Francis Ford Coppola), **THX 1138** (1970, George Lucas), **The Godfather** (1971, Francis Ford Coppola), **American Graffiti** (1973, George Lucas), **The Godfather Part II** (1974, Francis Ford Coppola), and **Crumb** (1995, Terry Zwigoff). Murch also directed and co-wrote the film **Return to Oz**, 1985. He has been an editor of feature films since 1972, and a re-recording mixer for feature films since 1969.

interview

It is completely improbable that film editing should exist! Imagine the situation a hundred years ago, right after film had been invented. When you went to the cinema, the films you saw consisted only of a single shot: there was no editing. The Lumière Brothers' **Arrival of a Train** (1895) was simply that: a train pulling into a station. Nonetheless, people were overwhelmed, and came back again and again to experience this miracle. Then, shortly after the turn of the century, the idea of cutting from one perspective to another began to be investigated, primarily by Edwin Porter in his **Life of an American Fireman** and then more famously in 1903 in **The Great Train Robbery**. Porter discovered that it was mechanically possible to cut film so that it would switch, instantly, from one image to another: say, a wide frontal shot to a side-angle. Not only that, but somehow – if certain rules were followed – the apparent continuity of space and time would be maintained. When you stop to think about it, this is astonishing, because for all human existence (and probably

for millions of years before that) we and our distant ancestors have looked at the world continuously. Every morning we open our eyes and for the next 16 hours – we get up, eat breakfast, get dressed, go outside – every step we take, every moment we experience, is registered and there are no cuts: what we see is a single 16-hour "shot." It is as if we took the lens cap off the camera and exposed 16 hours of film. So it would not have been surprising, in retrospect, if film editing had been attempted and found to induce a kind of seasickness in audiences exposed to it. That would be perfectly reasonable! Because nothing in millions of years of our evolutionary, biological past ever anticipated such a thing as an instantaneous transition from one moving visual reality to another.

The key, I think, to understanding why film editing is in fact not only possible, but glorious is to examine the cinematic quality of dreams, rather than waking reality. People have been recording their dreams for many thousands of years, long before the invention of cinema, and they all have in common these sudden transitions from perspective to perspective, from place to place, and from one time frame to another. Dreams do not have any of the inertia of physical reality: "I was in the middle of the jungle and then suddenly there I was standing on top of an iceberg" – that can be a dream, but it can also be cinema. It is cinema! I believe that the secret engine which allows cinema to work, and have the power over us that it does, is the fact that for probably millions of years we have spent eight hours a day of our lives in a "cinematic" dream-state, and so we are completely familiar with this version of

reality. It therefore behoves the editor to be aware of the miracle taking place when film is cut, and to seize full advantage of it. This means not using the cut merely as a way to articulate three-dimensional space, but as an extension of thought and emotion, just as in our daydreams, where we place ideas and emotions in closer, more "significant" and mysterious juxtapositions than would normally be the case. Of course the editor must pay a certain amount of attention to the physical space in which the actors are performing. You should not violate that without first thinking about it. On the other hand you need to push at it, conceptually, and always be thinking: "I've reached the end of what one shot can deliver and I'm now at the point of cutting to something else; how can I best choose the next moment that simultaneously intensifies and develops the emotion and that helps to tell the story correctly and which happens rhythmically at the right moment, just like a piece of music?" The moment of a cut is chosen very much like the entrance of an instrument in a piece of music. When the horn comes in, it cannot just blunder in; it has to enter on exactly the right note at exactly the right moment.

However, even if editing can be accepted as mechanically and perceptually feasible, in some ways it does not appear practically feasible. Let me explain: there is an incredible amount of duplication in the raw footage for any film. The director will shoot the scene from a wide angle and may do that three or four times until he has the performances he wants. Then the camera is put into another position, say a medium wide shot featuring two of the four actors, and the

(Pages 38–39) "The opening of **Apocalypse Now**, with its long dissolves and superimpositions, was not in the original script. In the helicopter battle material, Coppola loved the power of one particular slow-motion long-lens shot that showed the jungle bursting into flames. This became, on an inspiration, the opening shot of the film. There was also footage of Willard lying in drunken despair in his Saigon hotel room which had been shot as a 'character test' and was not intended for use in the film. The idea was then born of creating an opening montage for the film – a cinematic overture – that would integrate these two very different elements and get across the idea that somehow the end is foreshadowed in the beginning. This idea was further intensified by using the The Doors' song *This Is The End* on the soundtrack. (Page 39) What appears to the audience to be just one sound of the napalm dropping is in fact carefully constructed out of 15 different sounds. We could not just have a big amorphous bomb explosion. We wanted to hear the original impact of the napalm canisters hitting the ground, then the ignition with various subsidiary explosions and then the forest fire taking over, with exploding trees!" In **Apocalypse Now**, (1) Willard and Chef are in the jungle and the sounds get quieter until the moment a tiger jumps out: "Everything is simplified to absolute silence. Silence is tremendously important. Brilliant light is rendered more brilliant by the presence of darkness and likewise sound in a film has more impact if there are moments of silence."

1

2

3

In the scene from **The Godfather** where Michael (Al Pacino) goes to the restaurant to kill Solazzo and the police chief (1), Francis Ford Coppola did not want any music. "However, we wanted a sound to underline the psychological state of Michael so we used the sound of screeching elevated trains. The miracle is that the audience does not think there is something wrong in hearing a train so loud that it seems to be coming through the middle of the restaurant! The sound works because it is keyed into Michael Corleone's intense inner turmoil, the moment before he kills these two people at point blank range."

whole scene is repeated three or four times from this new camera position. Then the camera is moved again for another view of the scene and so on until, in the end, it is not unusual to have upwards of 25 complete takes of the scene from seven or eight different vantage points. Each vantage point generates two or three takes. So the editor, who is responsible for making all of this flow together, has to choose one of those angles he is going to use to begin the scene, and then decide which angle to go to next, and next, and next, etc.

The mathematics of this become quickly staggering in their complexity. I worked out a formula a number of years ago for the number of possible editorial combinations of even a few shots. Here it is: $C = (e \bullet n!) - 1$. "C" is the minimum number of different ways a scene can be assembled using "n", all of the shots the director has taken for that scene; "e" is the transcendental number 2.71828..., one of those mysterious constants (like π) which you might remember from high school. And the exclamation point after the "n" (the one instance where mathematics gets emotional!) stands for "factorial," which means you multiply together all the numbers up to and including the number in question. For instance, the factorial of all the numbers up to and including the number in question. For instance, the factorial of $4 = 1 \times 2 \times 3 \times 4 = 24$. The factorial of $6 = 1 \times 2 \times 3 \times 4 \times 5 \times 6 = 720$, so you see the results get big pretty fast. The factorial of 25 is a very large number, something like 15 billion, billion million – 15 followed by 24 zeros. Multiply that by "e" and you get (roughly) 40 followed by 24 zeros. Minus one! So a scene made up of only 25 shots can be edited approximately

39,999,999,999,999,999,999,999,999 different ways. This is fifty times the circumference of the observable universe measured in kilometres.

So when you are sitting there alone in the cutting room and know that tomorrow the director wants to see this scene all cut together and you realise that there are many more options than there are stars in this galaxy, how can you possibly make the right choices? Well, just as mathematics got us into this problem, mathematics gets us out of it – you simply have to start making choices. Like the old Chinese adage – a journey of a thousand miles begins with a single step. Once you choose where to start, that immediately reduces the options by an order of magnitude. The amount of remaining choices still looks horrifyingly large but then you think: well if I have begun with this shot and the actor mentions another person in the scene maybe I can cut to that person at the right moment. So now you have a reason for making a second choice, and out of the three takes available for this second shot you try to choose the one that seems to have the best light, the best performance, the best movement from the actor relative to how it's being used in the scene, and what you think the audience would most want or need to feel and know. So you make your second choice. Now this huge number has come down by another order of magnitude. Once you actually get moving, as with any decision-making process, things somehow seem to start to take care of themselves. However, the truth remains that editors are faced with a staggering number of choices. The fact that we can actually complete a film in the time that we have and make it seem in the end as

2

1

3

4

5

6

7

8

When film was invented the audience was amazed by simply watching one shot for as long as it lasted with no cuts – see **Arrival of a Train**, 1895 (4), by the Lumière brothers (1). Later, film-makers began to cut together scenes to create a narrative. Each scene was shot from one camera position with no cuts – see **The Great Train Robbery**, 1903, (6), by Edwin S. Porter (5). Then it was discovered that you could cut in close-ups without disorientating the audience – see **The Birth of A Nation**, 1915 (3), by D.W. Griffith (2). The boundaries of what an audience would accept and what editing could achieve were pushed even further by Sergei Eisenstein (8) on **Battleship Potemkin**, 1925 (7).

45

(1–3) In **The Unbearable Lightness of Being**, Walter inter-cut real archive footage of Prague 1968 with fictional footage (shot carefully by Kaufman to match the archive). "I added elements to make the material convincing that, in other contexts, would have made it seem artificial. I cut in the flashes of white film that you get at the end of a roll of film. I added the noise of microphones being handled roughly and the sound of tape recorders being turned off while recording. Ironically, these artifices made you feel that the footage had not been tampered with and that it was more real than it would otherwise have been."

if this is the way it was always intended to be is a little short of miraculous really when you come to think about it.

Once you have sorted out the picture, you are then faced with the equally gigantic task of constructing the soundtrack for your film. The helicopter battle sequence in **Apocalypse Now** is an extreme example of this process, but instructive precisely because it was so extreme. Like almost every war film that there is, the soundtrack recorded at the time of filming merely served as a guide. Only fragments of it could be used in the finished film because Francis Ford Coppola had made the correct artistic decision to use real helicopters and have the actors actually flying around during the battle. As a result, the motor noise was so overwhelming that it rendered the dialogue unintelligible, not to mention any of the other sounds.

I would say at least 95% of the sound in the helicopter sequence had to be completely recreated. Where do you start when you have to recreate everything from scratch? Well like all things, it becomes easier when you break it down into smaller bits. So we do what mural painters do. They mark off the space to be painted into a series of grids and then reproduce the appropriate part of the mural in each grid, like a kind of jigsaw puzzle. So, for instance, we would follow the helicopter "thread", forgetting everything else for the moment, compiling a list of helicopter sounds to be collected for each "grid" or section of this immense sequence: what kind of helicopter is it? How fast is it going? From which direction? How close? Etc. The question then becomes: where

are you going to get these sounds? From sound effects libraries, or original recordings? In **Apocalypse Now** almost nothing comes from libraries because this was a film about the Vietnam War, which had a different sound than previous wars, and Francis wanted us to be faithful to that sound. We couldn't use recordings from the Korean or the Second World War, not only because the weapons were different, and consequently sounded different, but because we were mixing in six-track stereo, and we had to have sounds that were recorded in stereo. This was in 1977–78, and at that time there were very few stereo recordings of any kind in sound effects libraries. So we phoned up the US Coast Guard, who were planning a helicopter training day at one of their bases in Washington State. It turned out they were very co-operative and allowed us to come up with our recorders and our "grocery list" of helicopter sound and get everything that we needed in original stereo recordings, with the correct helicopters at the correct perspectives. The same process applied to all other sound "threads" in the helicopter sequence: the munitions, the small arms fire, the footsteps, the off-screen dialogue of the soldiers, etc. In fact, as you might imagine, this extremely complicated and detailed process continued throughout the whole film. It was like making beaches out of grains of sand: you just drop grain after grain, and eventually you have enough of them to make a beach. What the audience ultimately hears is the result of this "granulation" of the soundtrack but, of course, everything is superimposed on everything else, and so the granularity is not noticed. For instance, in one particularly dense section we have helicopters, we have Russian AK47s, the artillery from

1

editing & post-production

(1–3) **The English Patient:** "For each set-up I choose one, two or three frames that represent, in my opinion, what that set-up is all about. I take photographs of these frames and have them on the wall when I am cutting a scene (3). When I feel I need to cut to a new shot I look at the wall and choose a moment pictorially. Each picture is marked with a number that tells me where to find that shot."

● <u>Desert Wreck 1938</u> • Last car loaded up, Katharine stays behind | **78** |

| **852** | Scene 78 SIDE < (MC2S) KATHERINE AND MADOX in car joined by ALMASY | | Side < M2S Katherine and Madox in the truck . Almasy enters frame >>>, "We planned badly". |

4	42	Madox and K and Almasy "we planned badly"	Almasy in to talk to K and Madox **114**
297 • 102			Good performances from all concerned **142**
7	43	Madox and K and Almasy "we planned badly" • Almasy's voice is a little more open.	Nice pause before 'we planned badly' **172**
297 • 145			Good look to Berman from Madox **178**
8	45	Madox and K and Almasy "we planned badly" • OK, pretty much the same • what about her.	OK readings, as if thinking them not as reciting **220**
297 • 189			Also good look to Berman **224**

| **853** | Scene 78 REVERSE< (MCU2S)KATHERINE,Featuring MADOX in truck. | | Reverse MCU 2S Katherine ,featuring Madox yelling out "Bermann ..." |

2	43	comp of previous • SGMTC	OK, but... **250**
297 • 235			
5	37	Good profile of Madox after 'Berman'	*Almasy is not in frame in this nor previous take*
297 • 279			K looks at Almasy **303**

| **854 A** | Scene 78 (M2S- WS) BERMAN AND BOY, TRACK BACK W/ BERMAN jumps in truck,They | | M2S Berman and boy ,track back to truck as Berman hops on it. They drive away in BG while Almasy and boy remain in foreground. Car |

1	99	Berman talking to his boyfriend, and sudden turn >>> the boy bows and Berman punches him in mock something. Car dries off over crest of hill, stops.	*Cutting them at the BB*
297 • 317			Sudden move to looking os >> **339**
			They boy bows to Berman **347**
			Berman mock punches him **348**
			Dolly back with Berman to reveal truck starting. Aim to >>> **355**
			Truck stalls but not see why at crest of hill **386**
			Almasy and Gayrab walk to it. **395**

| **854 B** | Scene 78 (MS) TRUCK drives away up the hill. | | MS truck drives away up the hill and gets stuck. |

1	67	Honzon, and poor camera move to reveal car >>> and car stalls in sand	See truck in single med bouncing and digging itself in **457**
297 • 417			Almasy enters >>>> **466**
			K out of cab **471**

| **855 A** | Scene 78 (MCU) ALMASY Looks at truck driving away | | MCU Almasy exits camera <<<. |

4	49	Close on Almasy - watching the car stall out, doing his little 'takes' and then exiting <<<	Wrinkled brow throughout **512**
297 • 485			Too much mugging **522**
			Exit with a sigh << **530**

| **855 B** | Scene 78 (M2S) ALMASY AND BOY | | M2S Almasy and Boy exit camera <<< |

| 4 | 52 | Wider on almasy, with great sand landscape in bg - the homozexual arab joins him and they both exit <<< | Gayrab enter <<< and look < at os car **554** |
| 297 • 535 | | | They both exit < **583** |

| **856** | Scene 78 STEADYCAM CAM (MCU-WS) WHEEL stuck in sand,KATHERINE exits, camera | | Steadycam shot,MCU wheel stuck in sand Katherine exits car Pan <<< She walks away from group exits camera >>> Truck starts |

4	126	Tire stuck, does not spin . fake . She weighs about 100 pounds . why would her getting out make a difference? They push car out . cut before the car is gone over horizon . She is talking 'bright' when she exits about husband 'rescuing'	A few rolling attemps **612**
297 • 588			Then see her out (camera not good at beginning of move) **617**
			"I'll stay" dialogue with bad overlaps **626**
			Can't understand her **638**
			"Come and rescue us" with a Gwen Scott **655**
			She exits > **658**
			Hold on wide of car with men around **663**
			Men push the car out **673**
			Almasy watches, back to us, disconcerted **699**
			Car off, but no exit **710**
6	132	better but no spin, why not??? can't understand what she says	Better camera for her getting out of car **753**
297 • 715			Better "I stay behind' **758**
			Better her dialogue until "Clearly isn't room for all of us" **772**
			Good lookback as she exits > **792**
			Almasy more in line with the truck, watching it 3:1 **828**
			Good scratch head as he turns to look at her os > **839**
8	111	Same problem with wheel • she is better, more understandable • almasy looks off after her . he waves to car and then does a weird DDL thing with his arms.	Ok camera her out of car **866**
297 • 848			OK dialogue compared to previous takes except "Clearly . " **904**
			Better see Almasy looking os > at K after truck freed **927**
			Better alignment of Almasy and truck, see him profile on horizon **942**
			Little awkward gesture as truck takes off (DDL) **950**	Good

| **857** | Scene 78 PAN<<< w/ MADOX as he exits car, | | PAN <<< witk Madox as he exits car Steady Cam Madox and group M "Certainly Not", K " I insist" |

1	27	Madox out . just for "Certainly not"	Madox out of car **009**	Good
298 • 006			Good "Certainly not" his face in the red sun **016**
			Berman voice clearest **017**

| 2 | 29 | Good 'certainly not' better than previous | Good look with 'certainly not' **044** | Good too |
| 298 • 028 | | | Good "no you can't" sotto voce but ok **048** |

| **858** | Scene 78 (MS) MADOX and GROUP,truck leaves in BG, hold on (MCS) ALMASY in FG. | | (MS) MADOX and Group in front of the truck,they lighten load and push truck away. Hold on Almasy in FG. |

3	100	Close on Madox already out . Almasy into the same shot, and Madox touches him as he leaves . Good pushing, with Almasy in close foreground . Car actually goes all the way over, but Almasy does that weird arm thing.	Both men look >> at her, heavy contrast **082**	Very Nice
298 • 058			Madox touch Almasy and then into the cab **091**
			Good Almasy looking > with truck in bg, cut at ST **122**
			And look > good as truck off in bg **136**
4	105	See madox touch almasy more . almasy waves to them, looking more at them than car. no weird arm thing, but a frustrated toss of the head . Good, and long sustain look before exit >>>	Three look at her (Madox, Al, Fouad) **187**	Only good for 3 shot
298 • 159			Good quick look from Almasy to her > os **190**
			OK Almasy looking at her os > w/ truck in bg << **208**
			Good Wave Almasy **222**
			Frustration, but no arm gesture **236**
			Truck has gone off << **236**
			Long long look at her os > hands in hip pockets **254**
			Exit > good **260**

852   297
                                                       .102

856 | 1:2   297
                                                       .588

853   297
                                                       .235

856 | 2:2   297

854ᴬ | 1:2   297
                                                       .317

857 | 1:2   298
                                                       .000

854ᴮ   297
                                                       .417

857 | 2:2

855ᴬ   297
                                                       .

858   298
                                                       .058
3

855ᴮ   297
                                                       .535

editing & post-production

(1) **The English Patient:** "At rushes I will take notes in a free-associative way about whatever comes into my head relevant to a shot. If I think 'banana', I write 'banana'! Then I look at the footage again before I cut a scene and I take a second set of notes that are more analytical and less intuitive. All these notes are all stored on a database that links the comments with the exact footage so that I can find key moments easily (Page 48, 2)."

the Vietnamese position, the small arms fire from the American M16s, soldiers calling out to each other, wind through trees, explosions going off in the background, fires and of course the recording of Wagner's Ride of the Valkyries blaring from the helicopter loudspeakers. It is the art of the final mix, which dominates the last few months of the film-making process, to take all of these disparate sounds and blend them at the correct level, equalisation, and spatial placement relative to each other so that the audience is convinced that there is a natural, organic series of events taking place before their own eyes and ears.

You read a book and the words are simply black marks on a white page: it is the job of the writer to evoke images and sounds (and smells and tastes). You see a picture in a museum and it is the job of the painter to evoke a sense of motion and sound out of still and silent images. There are certain battle paintings by Uccello where I can virtually hear the sound of the swords clashing, but that is my sound, it's the sound that I have supplied, provoked by the artistry of Uccello. The danger of present-day cinema is that it can suffocate its subjects by its very ability to represent them: it doesn't possess the built-in escape valves of ambiguity that painting, music, literature, radio drama and black-and-white silent film automatically have simply by virtue of their sensory incompleteness – an incompleteness that engages the imagination of the viewer as compensation for what is only evoked by the artist. By comparison, film seems to be "all there" (it isn't, but it seems to be), and thus the responsibility of film-makers is to find ways within that completeness to

refrain from achieving it. To that end, the metaphoric use of sound is one of the most fruitful, flexible and inexpensive means: by choosing carefully what to eliminate, and then adding sounds that seem at first hearing to be somewhat at odds with the accompanying image, the film-maker can open up a perceptual vacuum into which the mind of the audience must inevitably rush. The film becomes more "dimensional" as a result, and the more dimensional it is, the more impact it has on the viewer, the more it seems to speak to each viewer individually, and the more the sound can become a representation of the states of mind of the central characters – approaching the pre-verbal "song" that Stephen Spender called the base ground of poetry: "a rhythm, a dance, a fury, a passion which is not yet filled with words."

biography

Born in the UK, Anne Coates started in the film industry working on religious films. "At that time you could not enter the film industry unless you were in the union and you could not be in the union unless you were in the industry, so people started out in smaller companies. I did all sorts of things: sound recording, working in the cutting rooms and projection." A year later she joined the union and started to

anne coates

work as an assistant editor at Pinewood Studios. Anne cut several prestigious English films like **The Pickwick Papers** (1952, Noel Langley) and **Tunes of Glory** (1960, Ronald Neame) before going on to earn an Oscar for her work on **Lawrence of Arabia** (1962, David Lean). She returned to this film in 1989 to supervise it's restoration. She cut films such as **Becket** (1964, Peter Glenville), **Murder on the Orient Express** (1974, Sidney Lumet) and **The Elephant Man** (1980, David Lynch) before moving to Los Angeles in the 1980s. There she has worked on a variety of films, including **In the Line of Fire** (1993, Wolfgang Petersen) and most recently **Out of Sight** (1998) and **Erin Brockovich** (2000), both directed by Steven Soderbergh. "Sir Carol Reed said to me one day: 'I've worked with many really good editors, but I've never worked with one who cut with so much heart as you,' which is one of the best compliments I've ever had paid to me. I feel that is the way I like to do it – with heart."

interview

I was quite young when I started cutting in the early 1950s, so I did not know a lot about the rules and regulations of editing. I just did whatever I thought worked and people seemed to like it. I think I was always quite adventurous and I am sure that at the time a lot of the older editors criticised what I was doing. In the old days there was a standard way to shoot and cut a film. It was cheap, safe and static. First they filmed a wide master shot showing everything that happened in the scene, then they would move in closer and film each of the actors separately. Later when cutting the scene, the editor would follow the formula of starting on the wide, hold that for a while, and then go in and use the separate close shots. Editors would rarely cut on moving cameras. These kinds of formulas and conventions certainly did not apply on **Lawrence of Arabia**. For me, it was a great learning experience working with David Lean who had been a wonderful editor himself. For example, at one point in the film, Lawrence says, "We'll ride to Aqaba." Next we cut to the

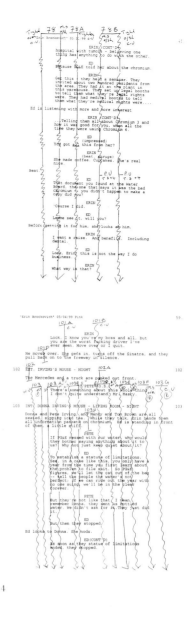

A marked up script (4) from **Erin Brockovich** and notes (3) taken while viewing the rushes. Each line represents a separate set-up or angle covering the scene. Anne had to choose from these shots when cutting together the scene. "I love new dailies and a new scene, though not always a new picture. It is sometimes quite difficult to get into a new film. Usually you cut a couple of scenes and you think 'oh my God, I've lost my touch, it looks awful!' Later you cut another scene – it looks beautiful and you get really excited. All films have their own life and their own heart and soul that you have to find before you can really cut." (1–2) "Music helps an enormous amount during cutting. You can leave scenes longer with music or a sound effect in mind. Nowadays we put music on a lot earlier in the cutting process during our temp dubs. On **Erin Brockovich** we used music from the film **American Beauty** as temp and then we actually had Thomas Newman (the composer) do the score."

charge on Aqaba. You would expect this scene to have lots of shots that you could cut between: for example, wide shots of the complete charge, medium shots of the various riders, close-ups of the horses' hooves etc. However, when we went to dailies we were amazed because David had done all the charge in one fantastic shot. The producer Sam Spiegel kept asking: "Where's the cover, where's the cover?" I said, "well actually Sam I don't think he's doing any cover." Indeed there was no cover – that was the only shot.

We did something on **Lawrence of Arabia** which is very common now, but was not in the early 1960s. We cut to sounds before we cut to their accompanying picture, so you would hear a sound before you could see what was making it. For example, sound from the charge on Aqaba is heard over the close-up of Lawrence in the previous scene. In other words you could hear the sound of the charge from the incoming scene overlap on to the outgoing scene and on to pictures that bear no relation to that sound. On the first night we screened the film, the theatre manager said to me "I know you were really hurried on this picture, but I thought you'd get the sound in sync." He did not realise that we had done it on purpose! We also used direct cutting rather than dissolving between shots. As a rule, when you moved in time or place you would dissolve or fade rather than cut directly. The most famous transition in the film is a direct cut between the close-up of Lawrence blowing out a match to the long, slow shot of the sun rising in the desert. I remember starting to cut it shorter and shorter. Then we took it to the theatre to look at it and David said "take it away and lose another couple of frames." I took two frames off and when I brought it back he said, "perfect". The cut worked because it helped enhance the magic of the desert and allowed the audience to understand Lawrence's infatuation with it. At that time, direct cutting was coming in instead of dissolves or fades. People were particularly going off fades to black. Unless it was done for a real purpose they reckoned that it took you out of the picture. The style of the French *nouvelle vague* was influencing us at this time. I actually got David Lean to go and see the French films and I think that was partly why he did those cuts in **Lawrence of Arabia**.

Lawrence of Arabia certainly has a slow pace. David kept shots on screen that I (being less experienced then) would not have had the courage to hang on to. He taught me about courage and doing what you believe in doing. If a shot seemed too long, he told me to wait until the music was on it and then I would see that it was perfect. On the whole I think he was right. Of course the film was re-cut twice before it was restored to its original version in 1989. At the release it ran for almost four hours and it did not make as much money as people hoped. The cinemas could only fit two or three screenings a day. There were a lot of logistic reasons why we shortened it. It ran for only two or three months at this full length before I took 20 minutes out. Seven years later I had to re-cut it again for television – I took another 15 minutes out. Although the film may have seemed long it was actually very difficult to cut material. In one scene Lawrence is greeted by warriors on his entrance into their camp. Both David and I felt that this scene was a little long and should be trimmed,

1
2

"The most famous transition in **Lawrence of Arabia** is the direct cut between the close-up of Lawrence blowing out a match, to the long, slow shot of the sun rising in the desert (1–4). The cut worked because it helped enhance the magic of the desert and allowed the audience to understand Lawrence's infatuation with it." At the start of the film you see Lawrence ride to his death on a motorbike. All you hear is the motorbike sound and an ominous sounding wind. "The bike noise was recorded from a real vintage Harley-Davidson. To get that particular wind sound, we listened to maybe ten winds and then mixed two or three together. It does not have to sound exactly like real life. We are making a dramatic movie – not a documentary."

5

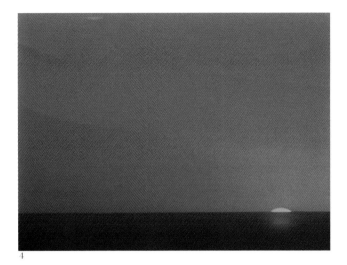

3

4

"**Lawrence of Arabia** certainly has a slow pace. David (Lean) kept shots on screen that I, being less experienced then, would not have had the courage to hang on to. David taught me about courage and doing what you believe in doing. The images were so beautiful. In the cinema you can see the sand rippling and notice all sorts of subtle things you would miss if you only held the shot for a short time." (5–6)

6

In **Out of Sight** the scene where George Clooney and Jennifer Lopez meet in the cocktail bar is inter-cut with shots of the love-making that follows. "I cut the scene in the cocktail bar as one particular scene and it worked beautifully. I then cut when they come into the bedroom, silent, as a complete scene, and that was so erotic. Then we started intermingling the two – that was really exciting to do. Then Steven (Soderbergh) had the idea of moving it out of order which also worked. There was a definite attraction between George Clooney and Jennifer Lopez. I do not think the scene would have worked if you did not have that chemistry no matter how much we had inter-cut it."

scene had a particular pacing and rhythm of its own. By trimming it, we had ruined it. So we put it all back again. You find that films take on a soul of their own and if you start playing around with them too much then you lose this soul.

On **Lawrence of Arabia** neither the producer Sam Spiegel nor David Lean went into the reasons why the changes were made. However, sometimes you witness major arguments about a picture when the producer doesn't like what the director is doing. As editor you are in the middle of this situation and you require a huge amount of diplomacy. Indeed if anything is going wrong with a film the editor normally knows before any other department. When the production company want to replace a director or cameraman you know about it. You can see when an actor is not giving a very good performance – and you know when you have saved an actor's performance.

On **The Elephant Man** there was a difference of opinion between the producer Mel Brooks and the director David Lynch about when you would first see the "elephant man's" face. There were really two alternatives: you could reveal him at the start when Treves (played by Anthony Hopkins) first discovers him at the fairground and cries; or else you could wait until later in the hospital when a young nurse screams on seeing his face for the first time. All the intervening scenes would need to be shot differently (either with the elephant man covered or without his hood) depending on when you decided to reveal him. Mel Brooks asked David Lynch to shoot it both ways so that we could use it both ways. However,

David decided that he definitely wanted to see the elephant man at the start and only shot it that way, so all the early scenes were shot clearly showing the elephant man's face and we did not have the alternative. Mel Brooks was actually quite angry because it was apparent that it would be better holding the elephant man back until the maid saw him. As a result, we had to cut round those early scenes and feature the other characters more so that we did not see the elephant man's face. There was a shot which panned across to reveal the elephant man and we cut it before you got there. We also blew up some of the shots so that the elephant man was blown outside the frame. When you blow up an image it gets more grainy and you lose quality, but since the film was shot in grainy black and white you could do it. Actually when I first read the script of **The Elephant Man** I was so upset that I thought I could not do the film. I still cry when I see it. It was even emotional at dailies. The first day after they shot John Hurt (who played the elephant man) with his make-up on, everybody came to dailies. David was quite annoyed, but when the dailies came on we started to hear people sobbing. By the end people had to leave because they were mopping their eyes up. Of course David was now absolutely delighted because people were reacting so strongly. There was definite emotion in the dailies, however, cut together it was even more emotional. For example, at the start there is a shot where Anthony Hopkins sees the elephant man first and a tear comes down his face. That shot becomes a lot more emotional when you see it cut together – even without seeing the elephant man. Another scene that was quite a challenge was when he goes to the theatre with Anne Bancroft to see a

"In the old days there was a standard way to shoot and cut a film. It was cheap, safe and static! First they filmed a wide master shot showing everything that happened in the scene. Then they would move in closer and film each of the actors separately. Later when cutting the scene, the editor would follow the formula of starting on the wide, hold that for a while, and then go in and use the separate close shots." As an example, these scenes are from **Above Us the Waves** (1955, Ralph Thomas) (1).

(2) **Out of Sight:** The computer proved useful as freeze-frames and jump-cuts were used throughout the film. "The freeze-frames were used to introduce the characters and to heighten little moments."

editing & post-production

"Throughout **The Elephant Man** (1–6) there are engine noises, Victorian sounds and a lot of humming background noises. You can use sound in a variety of ways to help dramatically in a scene." Quick shots of extras and buildings can also be used to add to the feeling and atmosphere of a scene. "They build up the story because they build up the movie. Usually we put too many in and then you generally single out the very best little pieces to build up. They are only quick cuts because they are telling a story quickly just to give you the feeling of the piece."

pantomime. It was shot as a straightforward eight-minute sequence. There were shots of the elephant man happily watching the pantomime to be inter-cut with shots of the performance. The scene simply did not work, it just hung there. So we decided to make a magical dream-like montage out of it – full of dissolves and different layers of picture happening at the same time. We took little bits from the ends of shots and bits from the beginnings of shots and we dissolved between them. We then took a shot we had of a black floor with twinkly stuff on it and superimposed this throughout the entire scene. We probably had four or five layers going on there. By some miracle it all worked!

All these dissolves and superimpositions must be shot as an optical effect from the original pieces of relevant negative. A completely different department does this, so the cutting room must describe all the bits of film that are being used in the effect and say what is happening and where. For example, at a certain point you may have 30 per cent of one shot, 50 per cent of another shot and 20 per cent of a third shot on the screen at any one time. This can be very complicated especially when working on film and you must visualise in your head exactly what it is that you want. Nowadays you can mock up a test on a computer so you have some idea of what you are looking for and although I have had some problems cutting on computer, it certainly helps when you have visual effects. On **Out of Sight** we would freeze a frame every so often, so the computer was a great tool to experiment with the effect before we ordered it from the optical house. The freeze-frames were used to introduce the characters and to heighten little moments, for example during the love-making. We also used jump-cuts on this film. Jump-cuts were popular during the *nouvelle vague* and basically involved cutting bits out of the middle of shots and making cuts that were not smooth. Such cuts can be great, but you must be very careful how much you use them, and you must keep the rhythm straight. It is the same with the freeze-frames. You must freeze it at exactly the right moment. It is very important that you do not lose your audience by overdoing it, by making them aware that you're tricking them. In the old days, jump-cutting of that style was very frowned upon. However, I have had a lot of praise from quite older-generation editors for the way that we used jump-cuts on **Out of Sight**. I think that commercials and music videos are mostly responsible for changes in the style of cutting. People can assimilate knowledge a lot quicker. Today you can see a commercial that tells a whole story in a minute. Audiences can now cope with that which they probably could not have done 30 years ago. Music videos have also led to very quick cutting and it can work wonderfully. However, I do not see the point of feature films with very quick cutting where you do not see what is happening. I like quick cutting, but I also like to see what is going on in the shots. I do not want to see just things flashing across the screen like a lot of it is today. You have got to see the shots to be involved in the story. The changes in cutting styles are for the better. But they will change and they will change again. I have always liked to experiment and work without formulas and rules, and I hope that I will continue to have the opportunity to do so.

biography

Cécile Decugis came to Paris in 1944, having spent the Second World War in the Alps. In 1952 she began university, leaving before the end of the year: "I had thought of studying history of art at the Louvre but my mother did not have a lot of money at the time so I could not afford it." Instead Cécile went off and managed to get a job as an apprentice editor. "In those days it was far from the era of video – every time you

cécile decugis

made a cut in the film a quarter of a frame was lost. It was the job of one assistant to actually cut the film for the editor, add black to replace the quarter lost and then join it up again." During this period Cécile would often go to the cinema, particularly the celebrated Cinématèque Française in rue de Messine which projected an innovative programme covering the history of cinema. Cécile began to cut short films including François Truffaut's first film **Les Mistons** (1957). She then worked as an assistant editor on his **Les Quatre Cents Coups** (1959) and **Tirez sur le Pianiste** (1960). During this period she was introduced to Truffaut's friend Jean-Luc Godard and edited his debut feature **A Bout de Souffle** (1959). These films formed the foundation of the French *nouvelle vague*, or New Wave, and are often credited with changing the style of editing. Cécile went on to work with Eric Rohmer on **Ma Nuit chez Maud** (1969) right through to **Les Nuits de la Pleine Lune** (1984), including films such as **Pauline à la Plage** (1982).

interview

When I started working in the cutting rooms during the early 1950s it was the era of the classic French film directors like Clouzot and Clément. In those days I mainly worked on short films, but then in 1953 I got a job as a trainee editor on the feature **Madame de...**, which was directed by Max Ophüls. I learnt a lot on that film. As the trainee I learned how the cutting room worked and how to make splices and organise the bins full of film. Around this time a friend introduced me to Claude de Givray who was a scriptwriter and a close friend of François Truffaut. This friend also knew Godard. My first work for this group was cutting **Les Mistons** for Truffaut. Truffaut was 27 and, although he may not have made a film before **Les Mistons,** I would not have described him as an inexperienced director. He was already working as a critic and knew everything about cinema. **Les Mistons** tells an enchanting story about the mischievous adventures of a group of kids. As well as filming the story, Truffaut also recorded a half-hour of the kids who appeared in the film as they talked naturally among themselves. He found this recording very moving. In the film we worked to cut little snatches from it under the images. I think he was disappointed with how this worked in the end because it was difficult to recapture the vibrancy he felt while making the recording. Often it is difficult to recreate in the cutting room what the director felt at the time of shooting. In any case Truffaut's universe was already clear from **Les Mistons** and he just burst on to the scene with that short film.

Truffaut rarely came into the cutting room because he did not like it very much, whereas you could not imagine a film of Godard's being edited without him being present. Rohmer was there all the time because he did not like you to work on a scene or even a shot without him being present. I remember that Ophüls rarely came into the cutting rooms when I was on **Madame de...**. Each day after shooting we would project rushes at night. Once or twice a week the editor would also show Ophüls a sequence that he had recently cut. He would then talk with the director and take notes on what changes would be made. This is obviously a much longer way of working when you are taking notes rather than the director being there. I remember particularly on **Madame de...**, there were two endings: one where Danielle Darrieux died and another where she did not. Finally they picked the one where she did not die. When there are two possible endings to a film everyone gives their opinion, which can make it rather complicated. I remember that we endlessly screened **Madame de...** during the evenings and at weekends, trying to pick an ending and to work out how we would get there.

In the early 1950s, before the New Wave, the means of shooting were different. They recorded on optical sound, which was a lot less flexible. The shoot would be a lot less spontaneous and much more planned. While people did shoot on location it was much more limited. With the new, lighter models of camera it was much easier for the New Wave to shoot on location – in apartments and on the streets – and be more spontaneous. This became the trademark of that kind of film-making. New techniques allowed a new aesthetic. Particularly before magnetic sound the quality of sound in exteriors was very bad. For this reason we would post-sync the dialogue in post-production by bringing in the actors. This was one of the reasons that a lot of shooting was done in the studio. Even exteriors would be shot in the studio against a back-lit transparency. A lot of lines were post-synchronised in **Les Quatre Cents Coups**. **A Bout de Souffle** was completely post-synchronised. During the shoot they started recording sound, but soon they gave up on it. In this film Godard picked the shots that he was using and he post-synchronised the entire take which took a fortnight. The actors were able to find the same spontaneity and professionals checked that the recording would match the lips, so it worked very well. The dialogue seems natural because we worked a lot on the sound, reconstituting all the elements that make up the soundtrack. So everything that you see, the police, the cars, everything had its own sound reconstructed. What you hear is the sound of the street and that was part of the search for what is real and natural which was such an important part of these films. It is very difficult and a huge amount of work to recreate what is natural,

1

2

3

cécile decugis

Another of the New Wave directors Alain Resnais (3), used editing to intermingle past with the present, thus exploring our memories and perception of events. The documentary **Night and Fog** (1955) contrasted the past and present in Auschwitz through inter-cutting (1). **Hiroshima, Mon Amour** tells of a French woman who has a Japanese lover. This Japanese lover reminds her of a German soldier who was her first love during the Second World War. As she watches her Japanese lover in bed his hand is inter-cut with the hand of the German soldier she remembers (2).

A jump-cut is when two shots are joined without any continuity – there is an obvious jump. This kind of cut became more widespread and accepted after the films of the New Wave. (7–9) Towards the end of **Les Quatre Cents Coups** the young protagonist, Antoine, is questioned by the psychologist in the reform centre. We never see the psychologist or hear his questions. Antoine's answers are just cut together and since they are all shot from the same angle there are "jumps" as you watch them. The New Wave film-makers shot in real locations with a small crew. Their production sound was often poor and as a consequence their early films contained a lot of post-sync. However, the film-makers tried to recreate the realistic sound of the street. All the sound in **A Bout de Souffle** was replaced – recreating the immediate sound of the street (2–3). In **Tirez sur le Pianiste** some scenes were post-synchronised and others were not (4). There is a three-minute scene in the bedroom when Nicole Berger tells Charles Aznavour that she has cheated on him. Truffaut wanted to post-sync the dialogue but the actors insisted that they could not recreate the performance (5–6).

certainly much more than we had done on the old style films. However, this style did not just come from the cutting rooms and the sound post-production. It was part of a bigger whole. The actors that we were cutting were also part of this. There was a naturalness in the acting and you could hear foreign accents. It was not a question of having the sound of the streets recreated while working with a rigid acting style. It was all part of the one whole.

As with other elements in the production, Godard and Truffaut did not pay so much attention to the pure technique of the sound mix. They were not so much interested in the sound being of a certain standard or in the established norms and conventions, rather they wanted to make it alive. They were against conformity in French cinema. What we cut had to be as alive as possible, appearing spontaneous rather than very worked out. Although often, that which appears most natural can require the most reflection. Truffaut was not so much interested in editing, rather he was interested in the idea of the film in general. He would return from a screening and say "that particular sequence is too long, you need to shorten it." He was fantastic with the overview of the film, but he got bored working with the detail. Godard on the other hand was incredible with cutting. For him cinema defined itself by editing, for Godard cinema is editing.

On **Tirez sur le Pianiste** I remember that we worked very hard – cutting until ten o'clock every evening during the shoot. The style was very different and I was not always sure that it was working. I used to always say to my assistant "let me know if it works." Then when we went to the first screening, Truffaut was very happy. It did not change because there were not many ways to cut it. I hate the term "first cut" because you should always be cutting to make it work. I do not think you should be doing bad cutting. After this "first cut" of course you will make some modifications. In New Wave films the cutting style was not planned in advance. They had a concept of what the style would be and they worked from a script, but they did not know in advance exactly where the cuts would be made. They would have been against being so pre-planned. This is not to say that we were going into the cutting room to find and create something new. The concept of the editing was part of the whole film like the style of the shoot and the acting. The editing does not exist in isolation. Sometimes in the cutting room you discover an innovation or you put right problems with the cut. However, in general what happens in the cutting room is a reflection of the film.

After we had done a cut of **A Bout de Souffle** there was a screening on the Champs Elysées. There were a lot of people present, including Truffaut and Rohmer. Godard felt that the film was not working and so we went back to the cutting room and started to re-cut the film. He used jump-cuts and had little regard for normal rules of continuity and this made the editing style very noticeable. I cannot say why in particular we used these techniques. Godard worked like a painter or a musician searching for what worked and often finding it. He was like an artist adding a blue or maybe a yellow and finding a balance that suited the whole. Of course the style of **A Bout de Souffle** has since become legendary, but before it came

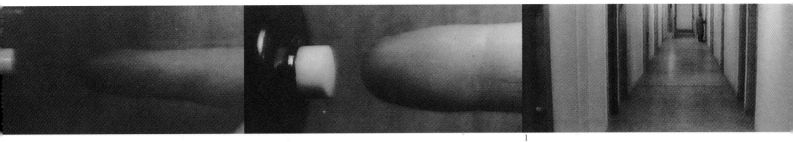

"**Tirez sur le Pianiste** is a beautiful film by Truffaut. I think one of his best and not because I worked on it. It has charm and it contains three ideas according to the dogma of the time." Among the striking editing ideas is the cut in to closer shots of the timid Charlie's finger as he is at the door of the impresario Lars Schmeel. Charlie is too scared in the end to ring the bell (1). When Charlie is in his bedroom and embraces the girl, the camera moves round the wall and dissolves in and out of past scenes before ending up on the couple (2). "This was rather a long scene and we needed to shorten it and find the right rhythm so that it would fit into the overall film. For this reason we did the long dissolves." In another scene the screen is split into three different images showing different versions of the same event (4). Truffaut at work on another film (3).

1

2

3

8

9

10

A Bout de Souffle featured a revolutionary style of editing. When two shots of the one subject are cut together without a change in angle the cut is noticeable and there appears to be a "jump". In **A Bout de Souffle** there were many "jump-cuts". For example, two shots of Patricia riding in the car each with a different background are cut together and appear to jump. Time has obviously elapsed. Also we see Michel talking with his friend – time has elapsed between the start of one shot and the beginning of the next and the cut is not smooth. The film also ignores established rules of continuity (1–5, 7, 8–13). Jean-Luc Godard (6).

Eric Rohmer (1) let shots play out rather than cutting. This sequence of scenes from **Ma Nuit chez Maud** is an example of how he held on shots. Jean-Louis (Jean-Louis Trintignant) is having dinner with Maud (Françoise Fabian) and Vidal (Antoine Vitez) (2).

out all of Paris was saying that it was a terrible and insignificant film. Many people did not like the New Wave crowd. **A Bout de Souffle** in particular was not liked because it shocked a lot of people – in fact at the time it seemed to upset the whole tradition of French film-making. Many critics were very harsh. People said that the New Wave film-makers were just making a joke. This was not true because they worked very hard and knew very well what they were about. The style may have been modern, but these film-makers were very aware of the tradition of film-making and they admired many of the older French and especially American film-makers. They had reflected on cinema and film-making for ten years before they began making films. There was no doubt that they knew what they were about. When you look at the films of the New Wave it is true you are much more aware of the editing, it is often visible rather than invisible. However, this was not totally new; the editing of Sergei Eisenstein was also very noticeable and visible rather than invisible. Godard in particular was very impressed by the Russian film-makers and their approach to editing. However, it is certainly true that the style of **A Bout de Souffle** was definitely a shock for the public – it was a discovery of something that appeared fresh and modern. Only recently a young 23 year old girl said to me that the characters and their relationships to each other still appeared contemporary. At the same time what appears modern and up-to-date now will be a new and different style from **A Bout de Souffle**. As Cocteau said: "All the revolutionary ideas in art become conformist after 20 years."

Eric Rohmer asked me to cut **Ma Nuit chez Maud**. The style was a lot more classical and structured. In the way that they view characters and French society and what they were saying there is much in common between Rohmer and Truffaut, but the way they say it is different. Rohmer uses long takes that have been worked out precisely in advance. He cut the picture quickly and spent a lot more time on the sound. He actually would go out and record background sound atmospheres himself, recording room sounds in his own house or friends' houses. To any scene he would add two or three very subtle and light atmospheres. They might sound like nothing when you go and see the film, however, they give it a very natural feel. Once a young recorder told him that he was the only director who you would see listening through the room tones and then going out to record his own. He was very pleased when he heard that! The use of sound is a modern innovation: if you are watching a film from 1935 you will accept the lack of sound but if it is a film from the 1970s or beyond it will annoy the audience if the sounds are not there. Kids nowadays all walk around with a Walkman listening to music and they are much more aware of sounds. Although I must admit the modern trend of having music everywhere, whether the restaurant, the car or the supermarket, is appalling. Rohmer is against this lack of silence. All of the directors that I worked with – Truffaut, Rohmer and Godard – maintained their independence and the notion of the auteur. The films that they made are definitely their films – and thanks to their intelligence and their integrity they are also very good and very important films.

biography

Paul Hirsch got hooked on film while studying architecture at Columbia. After being assigned a photographic essay by his tutors he was smitten enough to go out and get himself a 16mm Bolex and shoot 100 feet of film. The experience lead him to give up architecture and get a job doing deliveries for a small company in New York making industrial films for automobile products. On one of his rounds to the negative

paul hirsch

cutter he was offered a job as a trainee. After six months he had learned all about how the negative is cut and prepared for printing in the lab, as well as how to thread and operate a Moviola. With that experience he was able to get a job as a non-union assistant editor at a trailer house that cut trailers, TV and radio spots. "The sole editor there was overwhelmed with work, and he started giving me small projects like cutting down a documentary on **The Thomas Crown Affair** from ten minutes to three minutes, then I started cutting trailers and I was on my way. His first feature film credit was for Brian De Palma on **Hi, Mom!** (1969). As well as winning an Academy Award for **Star Wars** (1977, George Lucas), he has cut successful films in many different genres including comedy (**Planes, Trains and Automobiles**, 1987, John Hughes), musicals (**Footloose**, 1984, Herbert Ross), horror (**Carrie**, 1976, Brian De Palma) and blockbuster action (**Mission Impossible**, 1996, Brian De Palma).

interview

Years ago I heard a director quoted as saying you should only cut when necessary, which I thought at the time was silly. Now I have begun to see the wisdom of that remark and the sly joke imbedded in it. Who is to say when it is necessary? I have since developed a corollary to that guide, namely, make every scene as simple as possible, but not simpler. The trick is knowing when it is too simple, or too complicated.

On occasion, I have been asked to "doctor" a picture in trouble. In those situations, I simply watch it as an audience would. If something seems wrong, then I take note of it and try to fix it. Often because I come in as an outsider I am able to recognise when something is confusing. The film-makers do not see the confusion because they know the story. Once, I came on to a picture at the last minute and only had to look at the scenes that had been eliminated (i.e. the "lifts") to understand what the problem was. The director had cut out all the exposition – everything which explains who the characters

editing & post-production

1

2

1

"Alfred Hitchcock said we can structure the lead up to a terrible event in two ways: you can let the audience know what is about to happen and thus create tension – as in **Carrie** when the audience is shown the bucket of blood above the stage before Tommy and Carrie walk up there to collect their award (1–2); or you do not let the audience know what will happen and thus create shock – at the end of the film we are shocked when Carrie's hand seems to reach up out of her grave to clutch the arm of her tormentor/ friend (3)."

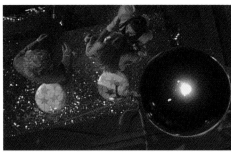

3

are and why they are in conflict with each other. I asked the director why he had cut all that out. He replied: "It's exposition. It's boring." I replied: "Well, it may be boring to you, but it matters to the audience. Without these scenes they don't know the story!" We put the scenes back, and the picture was a success, even producing a sequel. Other times you are cutting because you have to make structural changes. This was the case with **Ferris Bueller's Day Off**, directed by John Hughes. John Hughes was a writer as well, and worked in a unique way. He wrote his scripts in a kind of trance, working for hours on end, writing as fast as he could type. It was as if he was taking dictation from the Muse. This resulted in brilliant first drafts, so good that the studios would green-light his projects right away. However, he never did a second draft. He would shoot what was essentially his first draft – even if it needed a rewrite and even if it was way too long. For this reason, the first cut of **Ferris Bueller's Day Off** ended up at two hours 45 minutes. The shortening of the script had to be done in the cutting room. It was only after months of editing that it occurred to me that the events of Ferris' day off were in the wrong order. We had a parade scene early in the day, followed by a restaurant scene, a traffic jam, a scene in a museum, a scene on a boat and so forth. I suddenly realised that the parade scene had to be last. It was our strongest scene and should be the climax of the day. Then the traffic jam could be caused by the parade. Then the museum scene, which had been near the end of the day, was brought forward. So we ended up restructuring the movie and preview audiences responded favourably to the film for the first time.

Now to reconstruct a sequence of events like this, you have to have what we had in **Ferris Bueller's Day Off**: a story that is episodic and that takes place in one day. This meant that the characters were wearing the same clothes throughout the movie. Fortunately on **Ferris Bueller's Day Off** we were free to move scenes around with impunity. As a matter of fact, I suspect that Hughes writes his scripts with few, if any, costume changes just so that he can have that kind of freedom in the editing.

Although **Planes, Trains and Automobiles** didn't take place all in one day, the characters wore the same costumes throughout and once again we could make changes as necessary. The story of how we rewrote the ending of the film was a result of Hughes' unique way of working. The original end of the picture had Steve Martin and John Candy parting ways at a commuter train station in downtown Chicago. Steve gets on the train and departs for his home in the suburbs. He arrives at his home station, enters the waiting room and trips over Candy's trunk yet again. He looks up, and to his astonishment, sees Candy sitting there, having hitched a ride and arrived before Steve could get there on the train. Steve has been trying to shake off Candy for the whole picture. A dialogue scene ensues in the waiting room wherein Candy reveals his secret: he is not just a travelling salesman, his wife has died and he is alone and homeless. Steve learns he actually cares for this man who has been a thorn in his side and invites him home to share a Thanksgiving dinner with his family. There was a gag at the dinner table and that was that.

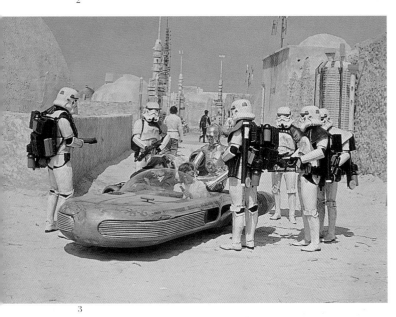

1

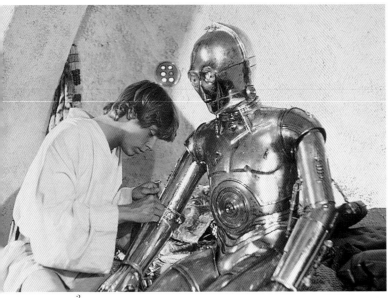

2

3

4

The scene in **Star Wars** when the robot R2D2 plays a message from Princess Leia to Luke Skywalker and Ben Kenobi in which she begs for help (4). "As written this was followed by a section in which Ben reminisces about the good old days, giving Luke his father's light sabre. Only after a good deal of time do they decide to respond to Leia's cry for help and this chatting seemed to minimise the urgency of Leia's plight. We restructured the film so that the playing of the recording came later, just preceding their decision to go for help."

The opening scene of **Star Wars**, which introduced Luke Skywalker, did not work and was dropped from the film. This meant that Luke was introduced later than intended. "The original cut had the opening battle in space observed by Luke Skywalker from the planet below. He then goes to Toshi Power Station to tell his friends about what he has seen. George Lucas intended the Station to be a teen hangout, but this was unclear without contemporary cultural artefacts. Trying to achieve it through behaviour alone did not work. Then there was a dialogue scene with a not very good actor. I argued that we cut it all. Thus we did not meet Luke until later in the film when we were brought to him by the robots R2D2 and C3PO in the Jawa droid auction scene. This lead to an unanticipated benefit – when the droids land on the planet, we have no idea who or what inhabits it. If we had shown Luke earlier, we would have robbed the planet Tatooine of much of its mystery. However, there had been a cut to the villains in the meantime, introducing Governor Tarkin, played by Peter Cushing (5). It was awkward introducing him before Luke, so we delayed that scene. Those scenes of Tarkin in his conference room talking to Darth Vader were manipulated. Some new lines were written and placed in Vader's mouth, easy to do since he was masked, and shots were borrowed to create new scenes not originally envisioned (2, 3, 6)."

paul hirsch

When we started previewing the picture, we learned to our horror that audiences didn't like Candy's character, that they perceived him as using and exploiting Steve. Then they stopped liking Steve because they wondered why he stayed with someone who had been taking advantage of him. We worked on making Candy's character more likeable, and audiences responded, but it was still a problem that he more or less threw himself at Steve's feet at the end and asked to be pitied. We decided to have Steve figure out the secret all by himself. We had shots of Steve on the train smiling to himself as if he were remembering something fondly; frowning and going through a range of expressions. Although Hughes had shot and printed over two hours of various angles of Steve on the train, there was only one take where he did this. Who knows, he may have been bored and decided to play something to amuse himself. We used that take as a basis for a series of flashbacks to moments earlier in the film when Candy had said something that hinted at his homeless state. Steve seems to figure it out, thanks to this wonderful take. He jumps to get off the train, as before, but before he gets off, we dissolve to a shot of the train returning to the downtown station where they had parted. We actually didn't have such a shot, but we simply ran the shot we had, of the train leaving, in reverse. Then we played Steve's home station interior as if it were the downtown station, since we had never seen the inside of it. We eliminated tripping over the trunk, as well as most of the dialogue in the scene. The effect was that Steve seemed to go back and look for Candy, who, in this construction, maintains some dignity. This change finally achieved our goal of gaining the audience's sympathy for Candy and the picture worked for the first time. On other occasions you want to create suspense when cutting and suspense requires the element of time running out. Physical difficulty alone is boring. You can show someone whose hands are tied trying to get free, but it's not very interesting after a short while. There's no urgency. However, if that person is tied to a railroad track and you show a train approaching, then there is a great deal of tension indeed. So to generate tension, you need to show that train coming, or the clock on the bomb ticking down, or whatever device you have at hand to demonstrate that time is running out. For example, in **High Noon**, the tension was increased with every cut to the clock hands nearing noon, when the killers were due to arrive.

In **Star Wars**, we realised the need for this time element while we were cutting the end sequence. Luke's task at the end of the film is a physically difficult one. To destroy the evil Death Star he must drop a bomb directly down a narrow "chimney". Obviously we all want him to destroy the Death Star. However, the scene becomes much more exciting if the audience also knows that Luke is running out of time. To achieve this time element, George Lucas sent out a second unit to shoot a number of shots of Imperial soldiers turning knobs and pulling switches (filmed in power station and TV station control rooms). These shots were then used earlier in the film to create a sequence (where the knobs are turned and switches pulled) before the planet Alderaan is destroyed by the Death Star. The shots were not strictly needed for the earlier scene because we could just have shown the planet being destroyed. However, it was our one opportunity to

Hitchcock was the master of suspense. He builds up the tension in this scene from **The Birds** (1) by cutting to shots of birds gathering in the background.

1

1

(1–3) In **Notorious** we know that once the wine runs out at the dinner party hosted by Claude Rains and his wife Ingrid Bergman, Rains will need to go to the cellar. Rains will then realise his key has been stolen and suspect his wife as a spy. The shots of the wine running out increase the tension.

2

3

establish how the Death Star's destructive power was turned on. Once we had associated this sequence with impending destruction, the audience would recognise it in the end scene. The audience sees the knobs being turned and knows Luke has little time because the destructive power of the Death Star is about to be unleashed. We have our "clock".

In this case we are creating anticipation followed by a climax. This is an effect that can best be achieved in time-sensitive art forms, namely music and film. Graphic arts (like painting) control neither the sequence nor the rate (speed) at which details are delivered to the viewer. Literature controls the sequence that the information is delivered to the reader, but not the rate at which it is read. Anticipation and climax do exist on the printed page, but are much less under the author's control, since the reader can simply skip down to the end to find out what happens. Music and film control both sequence and rate (or rhythm). And it is the editor who is instrumental in helping establish the rhythm of a film. I say instrumental, because the direction has a lot to do with a film's tempo. If the action is very slow, there is a limit to how much the tempo can be accelerated. Nineteenth-century music made much use of the device of anticipation and climax. This perhaps explains why this style of music has been so important in film scoring. The great film composers were all trained in the nineteenth-century style: Newman, Korngold, Steiner, Rosza and the great Bernard Herrmann. The work of John Williams is similarly influenced. This tension, or sense of anticipation followed by a climax, has to be created first in the script, then in the shooting, and finally in the editing. Hitchcock's famous example is of a bomb planted under a table at a restaurant. You can play it one of two ways: You can simply play the scene of the two actors at the table chatting and suddenly the bomb explodes, startling the audience. This will give you a couple of minutes of boredom followed by a start. The other way to play it is to show the bomb under the table at the beginning of the scene, and to keep cutting back to the bomb just sitting there, ticking away, until finally it explodes. The boring conversation is transformed into two minutes of excruciating tension with the audience dying for the characters to stop their blabbering and notice the danger at their feet.

You depend on the director to get the shot of the bomb, and you employ it in the way that maximises the tension. As for the rhythm, it helps if you shorten the length of the shots as you get closer to the climax, the explosion, or whatever it is. You start cutting tighter to the action as well. This results in a quickening of the pace, and increases the feeling of anticipation. I have used this device many times, for example, in **Sisters**, when Dr Breton has cornered Dominique/Danielle and he is attempting to cure her by confronting her with the murder weapon that she used. Their two close-ups are inter-cut with a shot of her hand reaching unseen for a scalpel on a nearby table. The tempo quickens, close-up Danielle, close-up Breton, hand at scalpel, close-up Danielle, close-up Breton, hand at scalpel, etc. and then, when the cutting is very fast, the punctuation is a shot of her slashing Breton across the gut. This was similar to the acceleration of cutting leading up to the destruction of the Death Star in **Star Wars**.

editing & post-production

1

2

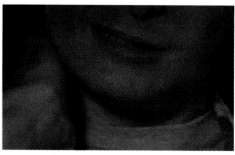

(1–3) The Secret of My Success: (3) "The song *Oh, Yeah* by Yello seemed perfect for the 'erotic' scene in the limo with its impossibly deep vocal repeating 'Oh, Yeah' like a kind of sexual innuendo. The filmed material consisted of Margaret Whitton coming on not-so-subtly to Michael J Fox, with visual puns like her lipstick extending like an erection, the windshield wipers erupting in a spray of water, etc. The edited sequence was so successful that Herbert Ross insisted on buying the rights to the song and using it in the final film. You must find the right music and then use the right image at the right moment in relation to the music. I try to make the action contained within the cuts appear to be animated by the music rather than simply cutting on the beats. I find that cuts seem more exciting and dynamic when they anticipate the beats rather than hit them."

3

MEMO "Hard Rain"

To: Mikael Salomon, Mark Gordon, Paul Haggar, Cece Hall

From: Paul Hirsch

Date: 5/19/97

Re: Final Dub Reels 1-10

Without patting ourselves on the back too much, I thought the mix sounded terrific. In a few places, we could be a bit more dynamic, especially with the music. These were the few notes I had during today's playback:

R1 SFX of truck motors going by in the street behind the Sheriff (We've got to protect the town...) were too low, although we must protect the dialogue.

R2 Perhaps we could delay the sound of the door closing when Jim gets out of the Suburban in order to suggest the distance between us and them. (A subtlety, I admit.) Important note: The music was too low when the truck gets stuck, and also at the end of the reel when the truck is revealed to be empty.

R3 The music was also too low during the jetski chase to the high school.

R4 When Tom climbs over the sandbags, outside the Church, we have an opportunity to play thunder just before he goes in the side door. It might help the transition from the previous scene at the end of reel 3.

R7 Doreen's line "I hope you're proud of yourself, Henry" etc. is out of sync. The thunder when Tom lunges at Jim in the boat is too low.

R8 The music cue following "They're witnesses..." is too low. (Mark Gordon thought the music just before Jim dumps Kenny's body out of the boat was too low.)

R9 During the first scene, the boat motor FX fade out before we cut outside. We should keep them up so that they connect up with the motor sounds when we do cut to the boats.

Another viewing might prompt other notes. Some of the sound effects could possibly be emphasized a touch more than they are, but all in all, the sound department acquitted itself admirably. The sounds are interesting and dramatic, the looping is invisible, and the overall level is exciting yet comfortable.

I am very interested in following through on the mix as well as the cutting, and I hope we can work out a way for me to be there when we complete the work. I think the picture is terrific and I am proud of my contribution to it.

5

EDITING NOTES "Mighty Joe Young"

12/5

2	Too much little Joe, shorten scene
	Look at Joe's response to Mother calling him
	Does little Jill blow one of her lines?
10	CU Joe just before he leaps at Strasser
12	Mother's death more powerful before - change reading on "I promise"
	CU's Joe while Ruth is dying too saccharine
13	Little Jill w/ Vern
16	Put title "12 years later" after fadeout & before fadein
22	Cat reaction to Joe - make connection
	Cut out sooner from R14
	Trim Pindi & men being convinced by Gregg
23	Trim R27a? - going into bushes
	Too long before chain hits humvee
26	Don't have Kweli say Gregg was dreaming
30	Does Jill know Gregg is tailing her?
	Make sure we don't think she saw Gregg watching her
32	Revealing Gregg - more of a surprise, maybe shorten
A32	Slow Gregg down
38	Stretch out moment before he says "That's a load of crap."
B68	Garth's "Whoa!" seems misplaced
A72	Lay in instrumental of Wind Song
	Extend Joe falling asleep
77	Trim end of scene
78	Cut Harry & Cecily after "You're dripping again"
	Re-examine slo-mo part of scene
	Banana business
	Show Strasser fleeing before T8
	Shoot CU Joe for between T18 and T20
83	Lose Gregg: "You got it."
91	Find or loop "Those are the guys who killed my mother"

A100	Lose "Hey! That's the monkey we saw on TV!"
B100	Look for "Go to the hills!" - if not, loop
102	Donald Duck
103	Too long before Gregg & Jill turn up
C118	Look at Joe funhouse mirror shots - too many and too soon
124	Can we sell FW stopping any better?
	Extend CU Gregg looking at happy family
128	Add cop giving money for Joe

6

The end of **Planes, Trains and Automobiles** (4) was also restructured to make John Candy's character more sympathetic. Using a shot of Steve Martin making faces on a train and inter-cutting with events that took place in the film, a new scene was created where Steve works out that John Candy's character is homeless thus evoking the audience's sympathy. The notes on a near final cut of **Mighty Joe Young** (6) and the memo referring to the sound mix of **Hard Rain** (5) illustrate the concerns of an editor during the making of a film.

Suspense requires the element of time running out: "you need to show that train coming, or the clock on the bomb ticking down or whatever device you have at hand to demonstrate that time is running out." In **High Noon** (1–2), the tension was increased with every cut to the clock hands nearing noon, when we knew the killers were due to arrive. The shots at the end of **Star Wars** (3–4) worked in a similar way. These shots had already been established as signalling the impending destructive power of the Death Star.

In **Carrie** you have examples of both knowing that "the bomb" is under the table and not knowing that the "bomb" is under the table. The prom scene is a prime example of how to generate tension. The establishing shot is a long tracking shot. It starts showing Tommy and Carrie sitting at a table. The shot then follows a girl collecting ballots for King and Queen of the prom. This girl goes from table to table and then out to the door where she kisses her boyfriend. There she exchanges the real ballots for the rigged ones. These rigged ballots are brought over to the desk where they are counted. We then see Nancy Allen and John Travolta under the stage. They are holding a rope. The camera follows this rope upwards and we see that it is attached to a teetering bucket of pig's blood poised directly over the stage. The "winners" are then announced as Tommy and Carrie. The camera then zooms in on the couple as they react to being chosen. The camera has completed a circle, ending up back where it began. The audience now knows the geography of the scene, where all the elements are. Tommy and Carrie are called to the stage as winners. Now their slow-motion march to the stage is infused with tension. We worry because we know that Carrie is going to stand directly beneath the bucket of blood. Without that long preface, the procession to the stage would have no tension, and the dropping of the bucket would have been a surprise lasting a second or two. Instead, we get a tense sequence that lasts several minutes.

At the end of **Deliverance** there is an example of a terrible shock. We see the still water of a lake. Suddenly a hand clutching a rifle rises out of this water without warning. This is equivalent to Hitchcock's example of the bomb being under the table and the audience not knowing that it is there. This surprise in John Boorman's film inspired the now-famous ending of **Carrie**, in which Carrie seems to reach up out of her grave to clutch the arm of her tormentor/friend. This shock works so well because the audience thinks the movie is already over. The sudden loud music also helps, and in fact, is essential. Endings are important because they are the final impression the audience takes away.

Movies are always likened to dreams, and I think when you are watching a picture, you believe the reality of it, as you do the reality of a dream. Then, when the picture ends, it is as if you are waking up. Just as you can only remember the end of a dream and certain strong moments, it is the same with movies. You retain an overall impression, but remember only a few vivid moments. The better the picture, of course, the more moments you recall. And when it is over, sometimes you wonder, did it really happen, or was it just a movie, just a dream?

biography

Jacques Witta was born in France. During the 1930s his mother worked as a script girl for directors such as Jacques Prevert and Marcel Carné. "My mother did not want me to work in films. She had to bring up three children by herself and film work can be very insecure. When she was working there was money, but when she was not we ate potatoes and water." Jacques' interest in artistic pursuits such as drawing,

jacques witta

painting and music lead him to learn the craft of book binding. But when he left college at 20 he knew few people in publishing, but plenty in film. A friend got him a job on a 39-part American series that was filming in Paris at that time. When the series finished Jacques was employed as assistant editor on **Mr Arkadin** (1955), directed by Orson Welles. He has worked with the director Jean Becker on many films including **One Deadly Summer** (1983). His relationship with Krzysztof Kieslowski started on **The Double Life of Véronique** and he went on to cut **Three Colours: Blue** (1993) and **Three Colours: Red** (1994) using a style of montage where the creation of emotional resonances is often more important than the development of narrative.

interview

There are three stages in the making of a film. First of all there is the writing where the director (or auteur as they are known in France) works in close quarters with a scriptwriter over a long period. During this stage there is no great financial outlay. The second stage is the shoot and the director is under enormous pressure with over 100 people involved and all working fast. The third and final stage is the post-production when the director once again has time to reflect and works closely with the editor. The third stage is like the first: two people in front of the material, moulding it. There should be a synergy between these two people and each should complement the other and add to the qualities of the other. For this reason certain editors can be great with one director and not so good with another. It is necessary for an editor to have certain gifts in terms of human relationships to be able to live and work in such close quarters. The editor must bring all that he can to a film and its director. A good editor will marry a project. He will enter into the universe of the film and not go off in a different direction. It is like joining an orchestra. Indeed editors are a little like soloists in a large symphony and the conductor of this orchestra is the director. The editor must be modest and humble enough not to want to make his own film out of the material – he should definitely not act like a frustrated director. Each film demands its own editing style or montage. So if you recognise who cut a film by an editor's style that will be to the detriment of the film because the montage must always be put at the service of the film. Every time I start to cut I have the feeling, not that I am doing a different job, but that I am taking on a new adventure. When I begin a film I need to enter inside it and absorb the material. The daily rushes screening is a way to get into the ambience and atmosphere of the film. It is important to try and have the rushes screened on 35mm film even if you are cutting video on a computer. The atmosphere is completely different between a video projection and a film projection. On 35mm you already have the feeling of a spectacle and of a film. You lose this projecting on video. For example, on the films of Kieslowski I would have liked to cut on computer. He however always wanted to project the film. He did not want to risk the video betraying his fragile and beautiful images.

Once you start the first cut, it is a little like working as a sculptor. You begin at the biggest in order to work down to the most precise. Often the first cut is long and loose. You have been working on scenes out of order because (for practical reasons of actors, sets and weather) scenes are not shot in a chronological order, but an economical order. At the first cut you suddenly see all these scenes together for the first time – and the result is often monstrous! Problems arise that have been there from the writing which then create a problem in the shoot and go on to make a problem in the editing. You rarely escape this logic – that the problem in editing is the repercussion of early problems. The editor is there to try and resolve these problems as much as possible. The editor cannot create material he does not have, however, his role is to try and extract the essence from the material he has. It has happened to me a few times that people have come out of rushes rather worried because the actors looked bad. However, at the end of the day these actors have been great because there were little nuggets among the masses of material and I used these nuggets in the final film. Nobody noticed these because they were reacting to the rushes as a whole. But in the end after trial and error and choosing the material, the actors turned out well. That is the magic of editing. At the same time the first cut is always very depressing and discouraging for a director. Indeed throughout the process of post-production I have often felt more like a midwife than an editor. That is because I have a director with me for several months and I comfort him when he needs comforting, and support him when he needs supporting. When there are problems with the production you keep his morale up saying "it is not as bad as you think, it is going well!" The first cut allows you to remove all the excess. To see more clearly you need to cut out the unnecessary scenes. Then you can work on the backbone or architecture of the film. This is done by re-cutting and making changes gently and slowly. Generally after about a month we get the first picture cut. It

There is a scene in **One Deadly Summer** (1–4) which Jacques would have cut differently if it had not been for the intervention of the star Isabelle Adjani. Pin Pon, played by Alain Souchon takes "Elle", played by Adjani, from a restaurant and she tells him "you will take me to a sordid hotel room and jump me." Jacques wanted to concentrate on a close-up of Souchon showing his reaction. "However, Adjani saw the cut and made me go back and use a two shot (1)."

1

2

3

Jacques worked as assistant editor on **Mr Arkadin** (1), directed by and starring Orson Welles. "I was only 20 and Welles, at 35, was someone to be venerated. He was not in the cutting room every day, although I remember that he cut one reel completely by himself. For Welles the important part was the shoot, although it was very much shot with the editing in mind." (4) "In the majority of cases the music is recorded once the cut has been completed. However, with something like the concert in **The Double Life of Véronique** the music will be recorded before the shoot and played back during filming. The music is then very much fixed. Since **Three Colours: Blue** was about composing music, it was pre-recorded and even played during rehearsals to create atmosphere (3). The music for the modelling show in **Three Colours: Red** (2) was also pre-recorded and played back so the actors could get the rhythm."

4

99. RUE PARISIENNE. EXT. AUBE.   99

Une aube d'hiver, les rues encore sombres et desertes. ALESSANDRO
et VERONIQUE vus de dos - pano sur les deux têtes, au fond une rue
en perspective. Ils marchent lentement côte à côte, nous ne les
reconnaissons qu'au bout d'un certain temps.

Un homme apparaît au loin. C'est un monsieur entre deux âges,
élégant, en manteau gris à col de fourrure. De loin nous le
voyons un bon moment entre VERONIQUE et ALESSANDRO : il
avance aussi lentement qu'eux, les croise et disparaît. VERONIQUE
s'arrête et regarde après lui - elle se tourne donc vers la caméra.
Elle rit, ou plutôt pouffe de rire. ALESSANDRO s'arrête aussi,
regarde dans la même direction, étonné de la réaction de
VERONIQUE.

                          VERONIQUE
              J'ai pensé... quand il s'est approché j'étais sure qu'il
              allait ouvrir son manteau et nous montrer...

VERONIQUE fait une démonstration de ce geste.

100. APPARTEMENT D'ALESSANDRO. INT. SOIR. NUIT.   100

Un appartement spacieux, meublé d'une façon non encombrante.
VERONIQUE se réveille dans un lit immense. Elle est seule dans ce
grand lit et s'assied un tantinet inquiète. De loin une musique
indiscernable. La caméra quitte la chambre où dormait VERONIQUE,
traverse d'autres pièces et couloirs et se dirige visiblement vers la
musique - que nous entendons de mieux en mieux.

A l'autre bout de l'appartement, dans une pièce aux larges fenêtres
qui peut être un atelier, la caméra retrouve ALESSANDRO assis à
une table longue et large. Il est penché, absorbé par son travail. La
musique retentit très fort de sa chaîne Hi-Fi : un orchestre exécute
le morceau que nous connaissons déjà.

La caméra s'approche d'ALESSANDRO et s'arrête. ALESSANDRO
sursaute : les mains de VERONIQUE se posent sur ses épaules et
VERONIQUE entre dans le champ de la caméra. Elle se penche sur
ALESSANDRO pour voir ce qu'il fait. Nous ne voyons que des gestes
précis, minutieux, sans toutefois savoir à quoi il est occupé.

9/10/90   Scénario de tournage   9 1

VERONIQUE, elle, le comprend avant nous. Elle a l'air surprise, sourit
brièvement et de nouveau fronce les sourcils.

                          VERONIQUE
              Alessandro...

Sur la table il y a deux grandes marionnettes. Toutes les deux ont le
visage de VERONIQUE, ou si l'on veut, celui de WERONIKA. Elles sont
en tunique blanche, jupe noire et veste. ALESSANDRO est en train
d'ajuster leurs vêtements. Il sourit à VERONIQUE.

                          ALESSANDRO
              C'est bientôt Noël, et je te voulais... Si tu ne les aimes pas
              j'en ferai un spectacle. L'histoire d'une chanteuse...
                          VERONIQUE
              Pourquoi... Pourquoi deux ?

ALESSANDRO regarde VERONIQUE. Peut être voudrait-il dire
davantage, mais il dit seulement :

                          ALESSANDRO
              Elles deviennent vite sales. Pendant le spectacle,
              quand je les touche, elle se salissent, elles s'usent...

Ils se taisent un moment en regardant les figurines posées sur la
table. ALESSANDRO soulève l'une d'elles, saisit les fils pour en
manipuler les bras, de l'autre main prend l'autre poupée par la
nuque. Comme dans son spectacle ses gestes donnent la vie aux
poupées.

**VERONIQUE regarde en silence la marionnette qu'ALESSANDRO
manipule au rythme de la musique, fascinée.** *

La voix sur la bande arrive au moment où ce concert-là s'était
arrêté : on sent une tension dans cette voix qui se met à trembler.
Mais elle surmonte la phase critique et continue pendant quelques
secondes : paisiblement.
Sur le chant, la caméra s'éloigne.

* Modification 4eme version.

9/10/90   Scénario de tournage   9 2

SEQ. 100 NOUVEAUX DIALOGUES POUR LA DEUXIEME VERSION

VERONIQUE sort de la salle de bains. ALEXANDRE n'est pas là. Elle entend le bruit
d'une machine à écrire. Avant d'entrer dans la chambre où ALEXANDRE doit être en
train de travailler, elle hésite visiblement. Elle entre, pose ses mains sur les épaules
d'ALEXANDRE. Surpris, il arrête d'écrire, se tourne vers elle. Il sourit. Il renifle, la
sent.

         ALEXANDRE : T'as pris ton bain? Tu t'es lavé les cheveux?

VERONIQUE hoche la tête.

         ALEXANDRE : J'ai... une idée m'est venue, tout à coup. Tu veux que je te
         lise?
VERONIQUE n'est pas sûre de vouloir entendre la suite, mais ALEXANDRE ne le
remarque pas. Il sort la feuille de sa machine.

         ALEXANDRE : Ca commence comme ça... (il lit) Le 17 Novembre 1966 a
         été le jour le plus important de leurs vies. C'est ce jour là, à trois heures du
         matin, qu'elles sont nées toutes les deux; dans deux villes différentes, sur
         deux continents différents. Toutes les deux avaient des cheveux sombres, des
         yeux bruns-verts et le médecin dut leur donner à chacune une tape sur les
         fesses avant qu'elles ne prennent leur premier souffle et ne poussent leur
         premier cri. Elles avaient toutes les deux deux ans et savaient déjà marcher,
         lorsque l'une toucha un four brûlant. Quelques jours plus tard, l'autre
         approcha elle aussi son doigt d'un four. Mais elle le retira au dernier
         moment, comme si elle savait qu'elle allait se brûler ...

Pendant qu'ALEXANDRE lit, le sourire qu'avait VERONIQUE en entrant dans la
pièce disparaît. Elle recule d'un pas, tourne la tête. Elle n'entend plus, ou ne veut
pas entendre, lorsqu'ALEXANDRE dit :

         ALEXANDRE : Ca te plaît ? Ca pourrait s'appeler : " La double vie... " mais je
         ne sais pas quels noms leur donner...

In **The Double Life of Véronique**
(1–2), there were two versions shot of
the scene after Véronique awakes in
the puppeteer's house. In one,
Véronique reads a story he has just
typed of two girls who felt attached
but did not know each other. In the
second version, the story is told
without words, through two dolls
dancing to music. "Kieslowski was not
sure which he would use. In the end he
used both – an example of something
found through searching in the
'laboratory' that is the cutting room."

2

1

96

editing & post-production

will still be subject to modification but it should be the essential cut. From then on, all the specialists are able to start working. Once the picture cut is complete my job consists of maintaining continuity throughout operations by ensuring that there is always a link with the spirit of the film.

The editor works technically and physically on the picture cut, but once that cut exists we call on specialists who concern themselves with editing dialogue and sound effects and the final mix. We talk with the director and give him our advice about these matters. He will question us, for example asking what we think of the music. It is always collaboration. There is nothing new in this; it has always been this way. However, before we started using digital sound on computers in post-production the editor would have been responsible for physically preparing all the sound on 35mm film up until the mix. Now French cinema is becoming much more Americanised. Sound has become much more technical. Specialists do everything on digital machines. Also there is more pressure to work quickly in post-production because films now involve more money. The quicker a film is finished and released the quicker the money will return. However, while the editor may work less physically nowadays there is still work to be done on the film. We are there almost to defend the project. Having worked with the director for so long during the shoot and picture cut, the editor knows what he would want in the sound edit, in the atmospheres, in the colour grade and so on. There are many things to be done, but the essential thing is to be responsible for the continuity of the spirit of the film until it is completed.

This spirit of the film would have of course governed what you did throughout the picture edit as well because, as I have mentioned, every film claims its own montage. There are rules in shooting but not really in editing. I think that in editing everything is allowed. It either works or it does not work, but you can try everything. Some directors like certain types of cuts. For example, Kieslowski did not like something that is done a lot in American films which is cutting within the axis. That is to have a wide shot and to brutally cut into a closer shot of the same angle. I used this type of cut very rarely in his films because I knew he did not like it. Yet in American films it is something which is commonly used to reinforce a reaction or an attitude through the force of the edit.

Therefore how you make any single cut is simply determined by the overall nature of the montage on the film. You can have a film which demands a slow and smooth editing style with cuts that are invisible, on the other hand if you make a violent action film you will have short shots and the cutting style will be different because such a film demands a different style. In my opinion a good cut is a cut which you do not notice because it fits in with the whole. The rhythm of the montage should be like the rhythm of music – it should form part of the ensemble and not seem like something from outside. In **Three Colours: Blue**, for example, the shots are held for a long time and the editing has a slow style, but it is this slow style that is a function of the rhythm of the film and the rhythm in which the scenes are played. Establishing shots are also held for a long time. There is a close-up of a cup of coffee which is held for much longer than normal as we watch a

75 - INT. THEATRE - JOUR

LE JUGE appuie sur un bouton et du café s'écoule dans deux gobelets, il est devant la machine à café du foyer du théâtre. LE JUGE les prend, et passe dans le couloir. L'orage persiste au-dehors. Il rentre dans la salle. VALENTINE n'est pas à la place qu'il occupaient ensemble tout à l'heure. LE JUGE appelle, pas trop fort :
    LE JUGE : Valentine... Valentine !
VALENTINE apparaît au balcon, à l'endroit que lui a précédemment désigne le JUGE.
    VALENTINE : Je suis là.
LE JUGE lève les yeux. VALENTINE se penche par-dessus la rambarde du balcon.
    LE JUGE : Faites attention... C'est haut.
VALENTINE sort le journal de sa poche, elle le prend entre deux doigts et le lâche. Le journal tournoie dans l'air, tombe. Elle atterrit dans la fosse d'orchestre.
    VALENTINE : Comme ça ? Il est tombé là ?
    LE JUGE : Oui.
LE JUGE se dirige vers la fosse d'orchestre en faisant attention de ne pas renverser les cafés. Il ouvre un portillon. En passant devant le pupitre du chef d'orchestre, la voix de VALENTINE l'arrête.
    VALENTINE : Ce n'était pas un défilé de mode ?
    LE JUGE : Non. Ils jouaient Molière.
LE JUGE laisse les gobelets en plastique sur le pupitre du chef d'orchestre et descend. Il s'accroupit, replie le journal. Des mains de femme récupèrent les gobelets et nous voyons VALENTINE qui descend un petit escalier et vient s'asseoir dans un vieux fauteuil à côté du JUGE qui ramasse le journal. Lorsque LE JUGE, surpris de sa présence, se retourne vers le fauteuil, VALENTINE lui tend son gobelet.
    VALENTINE : Merci.
VALENTINE sent son café. LE JUGE s'assied sur l'estrade.
    LE JUGE : Pas terrible, ce café.
De la machinerie de théâtre dans l'ombre, une loupiote rouge allumée.

1

3

2

In **Three Colours: Red** there is a scene in the theatre where the old judge tells Valentine about an early love while he walks to sit beside her (1–3). Kieslowski did not like this movement and asked that the story be told while the two are sitting. Although it had not been shot this way Jacques had to make the story be told while the two are sitting. "You never see the person tell the story. I choose moments of reaction that corresponded to what was being said. This is the miracle of editing, creating moments that were not made to be like that, but which become natural within the film." There were also scenes of the break-up between the young lawyer and his fiancée which told the same story. The scene shot of the two arguing (4–5) was too explicit and left little to the imagination. This was cut from the final film where we learn of it from the judge and when the young lawyer finds her with another man (6).

editing & post-production

4

63

La pluie s'abat avec violence sur les carreaux.

74 - EXT. RUES DE LA VILLE - JOUR

AUGUSTE est dehors dans la rue, sous un grand parapluie sombre. Il attend. La pluie commence, mais AUGUSTE reste là cependant que tous les passants se réfugient sous les porches ou aux arrêts d'autobus. Ses traits sont fermés. D'un passage souterrain de l'autre côté de la rue sort KARIN. Elle est encore assez loin d'AUGUSTE, mais elle le remarque immédiatement dans la rue déserte. Elle ne fait pas attention à la pluie, s'approche d'un pas assez lent. Lui fait également quelques pas dans sa direction. KARIN s'arrête à deux pas de lui. AUGUSTE, très lentement, fait ces deux pas. Ils se regardent sans un mot pendant un long moment. AUGUSTE a les lèvres qui tremblent, peut-être de froid. Des gouttes de pluie ruissellent sur son visage. KARIN a les cheveux complètement trempés. Elle ne peut soutenir le regard d'AUGUSTE que jusqu'à un certain moment, baisse les yeux. À ce moment-là, AUGUSTE penche la tête et l'appuie sur l'épaule de KARIN. Elle regarde droit devant elle, ne le prend pas dans ses bras, ne le repousse pas non plus, elle est comme paralysée. Elle dit d'une voix faible, désemparé :

  KARIN : Je l'aime...

AUGUSTE semble n'avoir rien entendu. Mais sans enlever sa tête de l'épaule de KARIN, il dit à voix basse, presque à lui-même :

  AUGUSTE : Oh mon Dieu...

Ils restent ainsi encore quelques dizaines de secondes, puis KARIN se dégage délicatement et s'éloigne doucement. La pluie continue à tomber toujours aussi fort. KARIN s'éloigne d'un pas régulier sans se retourner. AUGUSTE reste sous son parapluie, la tête toujours penchée. Il sort de sa poche le stylo-plume et le jette dans une poubelle proche. Nous restons un moment sur cette poubelle. On entend des pas qui s'approchent, une main vient récupérer le stylo-plume dans la poubelle.

5

6

shadow move across it. In these holding shots Kieslowski is searching for a certain magic. He is also asking questions and playing a game with the audience.

In American films it would certainly be the job of the editor to make the story clear and understandable and to look out for things that are not explained. But different films require different approaches. For example, Kieslowski leaves all his films open to different interpretations. He allows chance to play a role, there are always things that are not explained. For example, **Dekalog 1: I am the Lord thy God, Thou shalt have no other God but me** is a story about a father and his young son of about seven or eight. The father and son have a close relationship. The son is always playing on his computer, calculating everything. When Christmas comes, Santa Claus brings the young boy a pair of ice-skates. Later in the film a removal company put a pond in the front of the house and the pond freezes. The child calculates the thickness of the ice with his computer. He then goes out to skate but the ice does not hold him and he drowns. In the film, Kieslowski does not explain why the ice melted. However, in the script the removal company change the heating system and thus the ice melts. Voluntarily Kieslowski removed this explanation. It is fantastic because you are surprised all the time. It is the same with **The Double Life of Véronique**, as with **Three Colours: Blue** and **Three Colours: Red**. In these films there were things that were explained in the script, but not explained in the final film. We left possibilities of interpretation about things that are not necessarily symbols or something premeditated, but simply

windows and doors that we leave open. This desire to not always explain everything and to not follow a totally linear structure allows the audience's imagination to work. There are moments where the audience must make a little effort to keep up with the story. There are things which were developed and explained which then become abridged so now they actually raise questions rather than answer them. Kieslowski liked to ask questions and that was his way of working. Some directors only give answers whereas Kieslowski often asked questions. He said that he was sewing seeds and that it was up to the viewer to interpret them. It is a little game like the mythical composer, van Badenmayer, who does not exist yet is often mentioned throughout his films.

In general the director in France has a greater say in the film than in the United States so we are free in the cutting room to do things differently. This is because, right or wrong, in France we have built up the idea of the director as auteur or author. The commercial film in France is a rather suspect entity which people mistrust. Producers or studios rarely force demands on a director because once they are producing a film, it signifies a certain confidence in the director doing his job. In France you would not see a situation where an editor cuts a film without the assent of the director like when Robert Wise cut Orson Welles' **The Magnificent Ambersons** for the studios. Although at the same time, while the director can maintain his right to cut the film, the studio can still apply pressure through their control of the release, distribution and promotion. In France there was a famous case in 1968 involving Edouard Luntz who had shot the film **Le Grabuge**

In **Three Colours: Blue** the fades to black throughout the film, often accompanied by orchestral music, were planned in the script and scored in advance (1–2). "At one point we even tried to do fades to blue, but I felt that was just too much!" Kieslowski often played with the viewer and posed questions with shots that would be held much longer than normal. He also searched for the magic in the light. For example, in Véronique's ball on the train in **The Double Life of Véronique** (3).

18

Elle allume une lampe, s'approche de la fenêtre, appuie sa main sur le cadre et regarde au-dehors. Par la fenêtre on voit le jardin, les vieux arbres dans la lumière tombante du crépuscule, l'allée et beaucoup plus loin Paris. La CAMERA s'avance, on perd JULIE pour ne plus voir que ce qu'il y a derrière la fenêtre. Le parc s'assombrit doucement, à vue d'œil. En l'espace de quelques dizaines de secondes la nuit tombe. Simultanément au parc qui s'assombrit, le reflet du visage de JULIE, éclairé par la lampe, apparaît dans la vitre. En même temps que surgit son visage, la même musique que précédemment retentit. JULIE ferme les yeux.

20 - EXT. RUE. IMMEUBLE DE LA COPISTE - JOUR

JULIE arrête sa petite voiture de sport, recule et se gare, non loin d'un café avec une terrasse donnant sur la rue. Elle descend et entre sous le porche d'un immeuble, on voit qu'elle connaît cet endroit.

21 - INT. CAGE D'ESCALIER - JOUR

JULIE attend l'ascenseur. Elle se rend compte qu'il est occupé, à cause de la lumière rouge qui clignote régulièrement. Elle perd visiblement patience et commence à monter les escaliers en courant. Aux environs du deuxième étage elle croise l'ascenseur, vitré, éclairé, qui descend majestueusement. JULIE sonne à la porte du quatrième étage. Une jeune femme lui ouvre, c'est la COPISTE.

22 - INT. APPARTEMENT DE LA COPISTE - JOUR

Dans la chambre s'entassent les partitions, les rouleaux de papier à musique et des vieilles estampes, dont la COPISTE est visiblement une grande amoureuse : il y en a sur tous les murs.

editing & post-production

Are you able to talk?

There is an establishing shot at the hospital in **Three Colours: Blue** which is held for a long time as a kind of renaissance and overture (3) and in the light on the coffee cup (2). "It is like an abstract painter looking and searching, and sometimes finding. The genius of Kieslowski was shooting material in which we could find the magic."

for Darryl F. Zanuck in Venezula. Zanuck was not happy with the edit and the case went to court in France. Edgar Faure was Luntz's lawyer and they won the trial. So Zanuck lost and it was ordered that he release the film in France. Release the film he did, but for one week only in a small cinema. Zanuck may have lost the trial but he won in every other sense!

This respect for the rights of the auteur means that audience previews are much less common in France. It is still a good idea to show a film to other people during the cut, however, we are more likely to do it with friends or people whose opinion we trust who do not know the film. For example, Kieslowski would not work without screenings. Very rarely would we watch a cut on the editing table in the cutting room. It would always be a screening with his principal collaborators. As soon as we had a cut he would call his director of photography Slawomir Idziak, his musician Zbigniew Preisner, his producer Marin Karmitz, his assistant director Emmanuel Finkiel, his sound engineer Jean Claude Laureux and we would project the film. Afterwards we would meet up and discuss what we had just seen. Kieslowski was amazing because he would not defend anything. He took away what interested him and we would go back to the cutting room and work together on redoing the edit. Then two or three weeks later everyone would be called back and we would project the film again. Every time we projected there would be some new people who did not know the story. This system worked well because Kieslowski was like a great conductor who knew everyone's strengths and how to get the best out of everyone. One of the great things about editing is the possibility of enriching oneself through contact with different people. In the case of Kieslowski it was truly an enrichment.

There is always a possible complete change between the written script and the final film. A scene that was fantastic in the writing might not be so good when it is shot. This may be because of the acting, the photography, the set or any one of a number of other reasons. If the scene does not work in the cut it can disappear. On the other hand there can be scenes that seem weak in the script, but through the direction and the performances they reveal themselves as being great. These are the vicissitudes between the vision of the auteur and the result. The film is a living thing and the camera is also like a living thing so often it will record something which may not be the exact reflection of what was written on paper. Then once you have finished shooting, you begin the whole process of editing which is magical and fragile and almost impossible to explain. It is like a painter trying to explain a deep blue he has used – basically you have to go and see it!

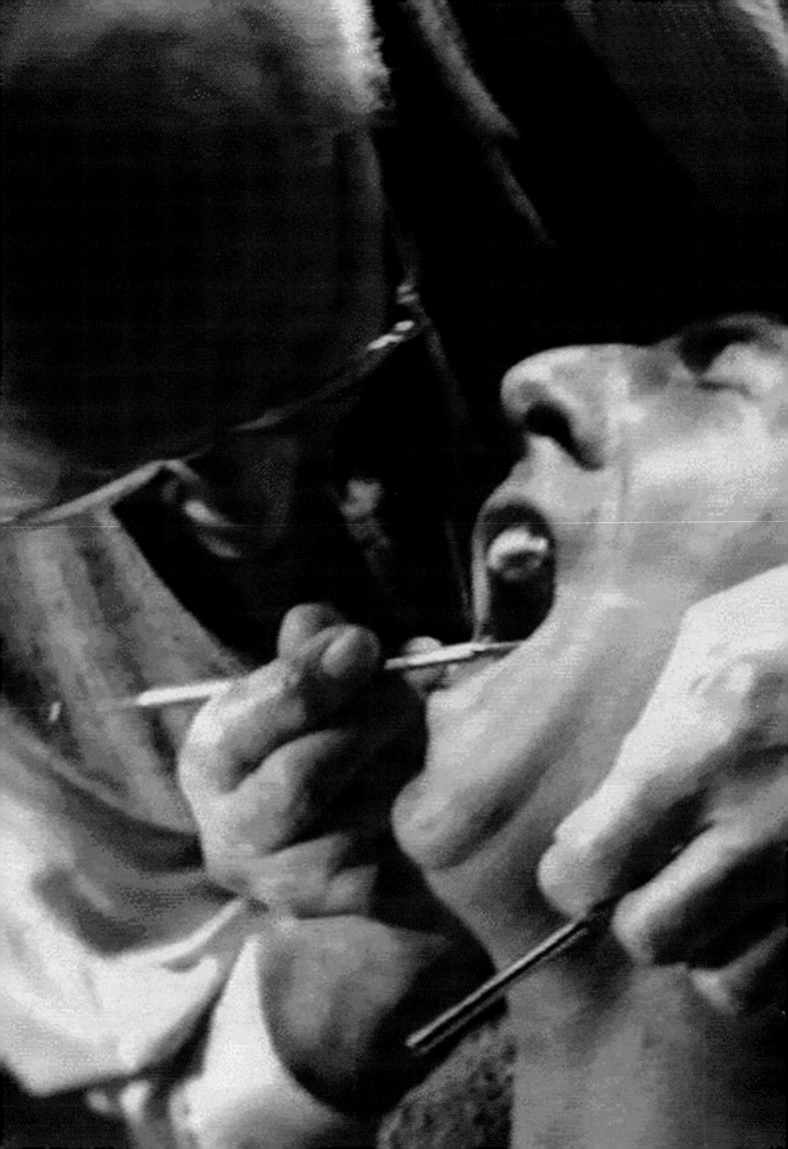

biography

Jim Clark became an editor through "hard work, good luck and determination." He started as a trainee in the early 1950s at Ealing Studio, London. "Getting that job was pure luck: I had an introduction to the personnel manager of the studio who said he'd call if they needed extra help. Fortunately after a couple of months they were short-handed and I was asked to start." Through a friendship with documentary film producer

jim clark

interview

Basil Wright, Jim got to cut a film for the Children's Film Foundation. "When it was over I was out of work, totally unknown and unable to get a job anywhere! I had a family to feed too. After a short period of reasonable desperation I found a job cutting puppet films for Disney – a more wretched, dispirited editor could not have existed at that time!" Jim called his old friend and mentor, editor Jack Harris, who gave him a job as second assistant on **The Prince and the Showgirl** (1957, Laurence Olivier). Through working with Jack Harris on a number of pictures, Jim met Stanley Donen who subsequently gave him a break to cut **Surprise Package** (1961). Since then Jim has gone on to work with John Schlesinger on **Midnight Cowboy** (1969) and **Marathon Man** (1976), Roland Joffe on **The Killing Fields** (1984) and **The Mission** (1986), Michael Caton-Jones on **Memphis Belle** (1990) and **This Boy's Life** (1993), Michael Apted on **Nell** (1994) and **The World is Not Enough** (1999), and Jerry Zaks on **Marvin's Room** (1996).

There used to be a difference between those who were called "editors" and those called "cutters". The late Elmo Williams, himself an editor and later a producer was adamant that there was a subtle difference here. The editor could be called upon to be more creative whereas the cutter just got in there and cut the stuff as quickly as possible for a lower fee. This may have applied more when there was a definite strata in the Hollywood studios: Grade A productions would be serviced by editors and B pictures by cutters. I like to think that in British studios the difference applied to those who were interested in cinema as an art and those who were interested in cinema as a paycheck. I came into a film studio as a trainee in the early '50s, and was astonished by the lack of interest shown in film appreciation. Few of my colleagues ever went to the movies. They could not discuss the aesthetics of cinema (one rapidly learned not to broach this subject) and they were interested only in their jobs – and keeping them. Most people around me had entered the film industry through

"I had no particular difficulties with **Charade** (1–4). The fun in making the film is reflected in the finished product which has an easy relaxed feeling. The main work we did concerned the finale in the theatre, where Cary Grant is under the stage and the villain, Walter Matthau, is above him on stage (2–4). Cary has to decide which trap door to open when Matthau moves. We were after suspense here and I had plenty of material to construct it. The sound of the footsteps was crucial to the scene and their elaborate recording really paid off."

nepotism; their fathers were probably in the carpenter's or plasterer's shops and had sought a position for their sons (most of the editorial staff were male) in the mail room. Eventually they drifted into the mainstream through whichever department needed a pair of hands. There was no real love or understanding of cinema.

All of this was before we had any form of film school in England. At Ealing studios (which acted as my film school) I can recall only one editor who displayed any real knowledge of film history. The war had, of course, played a part in discouraging this since most of the editors had been on active service, and prior to the war very few cinemas ran anything other than mainstream films. It was not until the war ended and Roger Manvell published his widely read Penguin book dealing with film appreciation that the public began to take an interest in film history. It was only the specialist cinemas such as the Academy, Curzon and Studio One that provided the outlets for foreign films – if one was lucky enough to live near London. Outside the capital the pickings were thin and thus the film societies, of which I started two, prospered until television moved in to gradually kill them off.

The approach to film editing evolves gradually and fine editors have emerged from a variety of sources, despite the lack of any formal training. I have never believed that film editing can be taught by example. Watching a film editor at work can be exasperating. As an assistant I would try and learn by watching, but there was little to gain from that unless the editor wanted his assistant looking over his shoulder into the small Moviola screen. In my experience editors were not inclined to become teachers, perhaps rather hoping the mystique would remain forever locked inside them and there was little interest in preparing the next generation. With the advent of digital editing the notion of teaching whilst working became more possible, and if the editor is open to the task an assistant may learn something by having the editor talk through a scene and give his reasons why he has done it that way. Provided there is no feeling of judgment going on, the editor can relax into forming something of a partnership with the assistant, graduating to allowing the assistant to take over certain scenes. I have found that when under pressure, a trustworthy assistant who can re-cut without wrecking is a great asset. This is not to undermine the importance of an assistant's own duties. Every cutting room requires good housekeeping, and I try to employ assistants who are red-hot at ensuring everything that comes into the room and into the machine is correctly logged. Now that we have digital systems this is even more necessary. An error upfront can be costly and confusing at the conclusion. A sloppy assistant is of no value to me. Although I am long-suffering and rarely lose my temper, anything that prevents smooth procedure is inclined to distress me – I would not dictate to the assistant exactly how the housekeeping should be done, but I insist on it working correctly.

No two editors or directors would edit a scene in a similar fashion, just as no two potters would give you the same vessel from the same clay. We are manipulators, often suppressing our personalities. In most cases the director is the boss (sometimes the producer takes on this role), and one defers always to that personality whose signature represents the picture – this applies to all branches of production, not only editing. The feature-film editor is employed for the nine-month gestation period common in feature production. There is an obvious human parallel, though in film the "seed" must have been planted long before gestation commences! The first three or four months will be spent shooting the material, the next three editing it and the final two in refining both picture and sound. Sometimes these lines become blurred depending on any number of factors: test screenings may reveal flaws in the film which need to be patched up and mended via re-shoots; or maybe there is a struggle between producers and backers, in which case post-production gets delayed. Whatever problems exist, they have to be solved before the final act of negative cutting, when, so to speak, the cord is cut. After that the "baby" is everybody's property and no longer the sole property of its maker (the director) who will however continue to be protective throughout the thick and thin of distribution and presentation. In the days when film directors were under contract to studios they were very often obliged to leave their babies in the hands of others whilst they got on with the next project. Their involvement with the cutting room would be minimal. John Ford once remarked that he sometimes saw his films for the first time when they were premiered. In those days the producers had a more active hand in the finishing process – the moguls had final cut; the directors were hired hands. That would be unthinkable today. Although plenty of good work did emerge from the studios in the "golden age" of the '30s and '40s (and a great deal of dross) when the producer was king. During editing I am very often first in the room. I start working directly, usually eating my breakfast with one hand and working with the other. Normally I am at work by 8.00a.m. and leave around 7.00p.m. – my hours are dictated not by work, but by the traffic flow, depending on where I am situated. In fact I find that my eyes do not allow me to cut too late – and I am constantly being told I spend too many hours in front of the monitor. Recently we had a large plasma screen in the room, which I used solely for viewing and found it a great help, both for myself and also for anyone who came into view – it turned the cutting room into a small multiplex.

Our role usually begins on location, watching the rushes from the previous day's shooting. I normally sit with the director and the assistant supplies me with a print-out of the daily rolls with space for notes. If the director gives me a note, I write it down, and always try to follow his directions. Naturally, at rushes one is looking for any problems that might show up such as scratches, poor focus, possible exposure problems, or marks on the film that could be on the negative, etc. I have never been clever enough to spot continuity errors at rushes, but I do occasionally question the cover that has been presented – whether there is more material to come since I never start editing until all the material is available.

Now that we are on digital, my first cut is very rough and ready. My system, if I have one at all, is to run the material several times, looking at the script to see exactly what cover I have and noting down any particular things that take my fancy

A very helpful development with digital is the ability to build up a section that contains all good line readings in script order regardless of angles: "If I had been able to utilise this when we cut **The Mission** (1–3) it would have saved us hours of work. In that film we had many long takes, each with many different readings. In post we built up rolls containing all versions of each line, so the director could whittle the possible readings down to maybe six out of 60. A very time consuming operation, and in the end it was hard to say what was good because we were word-blind by then!"

10

SCRIPT AMENDMENT 13TH APRIL, 1982

95.   INT. HALL DE RECEPTION. DAY.   95.

Flies and lassitude. A few days passed. Stubble turning
into beards. Everyone sprawled inside to escape the
afternoon heat. Fanning with cardboard. And MORGAN
spraying flies in the immediate vicinity. ROCKOFF laying
on his table-cloth. Heavily soiled. And socks a write-off.
He reads "Penthouse" slowly from the front. SWAIN next
to him reading a G Green novel.
An OFFICIAL with a moustache appears and somebody directs
him across.

                    OFFICIAL
          Il y a quelqu'un qui parle Francais?
Several do but nobody wants to admit it. SWAIN reluctantly
owns up.

                    SWAIN
          S'il vous plait, Monsieur?
He stands and joins the OFFICIAL at the door. A
discussion follows.
DOUGAL whittles a fork out of bamboo. McENTIRE bothers
a tune out of the piano. But the heat is overwhelming.
So is the boredom.

                    DOUGLAS
          Hurry it up, you read it daft.

                    ROCKOFF
          I intend to undress this
          magazine slowly.
More whistling and fly-spraying and yawning and fanning
and boredom. SCHANBERG shoves a cigar in his mouth.
Reaches for matches and gets back into his conversation
with SUNDSVALL. The DOCTOR makes the running.

                    SUNDSVALL
          I think there's some sort of
          internal power-struggle going on -
          there seems to be different groups
          holding different parts of the city
          - from what I can gather they're
          terrified that something could cause
          them to loose power .....
SWAIN comes back and interrupts them with a tense
expression.

                    SWAIN
          They've got some Red Cross instruction
          sheets they want translated. I said
          you'd give me a hand ...

                    SCHANBERG
          Pran reads better than I do.
PRAN gets up ready to offer his services. SWAIN has an
evasive smile.

                    SWAIN
          Actually, I think it would be
          simpler if I did it with you.

1

95.   CONTINUED: 95.

PRAN looks hurt. SCHANBERG looks angry. He follows
SWAIN to the door.

An opulent entrance hall. Sweeping staircase.
Chandeliers. Paintings imported from France. Like
everywhere else SQUATTERS have laid claim. FAMILIES
with CHILDREN billeted out here. The floor and landings
are full. SCHANBERG is pissed with SWAIN and snaps as
he closes the door.

                    SCHANBERG
          What d'you do that for?
          He's insecure enough as it is ...

                    SWAIN
          The Cambodians have gotta leave,
          Syd.
The tidings hit like an anvil. SWAIN bolts it onto
SCHANBERG's head.

                    SWAIN
          (continued)
          They want everybody's passport in.
          He wants everybody upstairs down
          here. All the Cambodians are out.

95 A   INT. EMBASSY DAY.

ROCKOFF is in a rage against SYDNEY, since without the necessary
papers PRAN cannot stay inside the embassy. SWAIN produces two
passports and proposes an idea.

96.   EXT.   GARDENS/COMPOUND, FRENCH EMBASSY.   DAY.   96.

Pandemonium out here. CAMBODIANS packing up. Some burying
valuables. Some offering them to the GENDARME. Emeralds
and gold without value. Cars stuffed with possessions.
Cars pushed towards the gate. An old van forced into a
cooking fire. Dense black smoke as the tank explodes.
Confusion in confusion. CHILDREN screaming after their
screaming PARENTS. "Mon Mari. Mon Mari." ROZA dragging
her GRANDMOTHER to her feet. Every corner of the compound
furnished with weeping and misery.
SCHANBERG battles the disorder looking for PRAN. Accosted
by a MONTAGNARD OFFICER. "I fought five years. I lost
my hand!" Tears his shirt apart with the other. An atlas
of terrible scars cross his chest. "I was wounded for
nothing. Nothing!" Impossible despair. Impossible to
look into his eyes. "Please do something to help us. You

2

110

editing & post-production

SCRIPT AMENDMENT 13TH APRIL, 1983

99.   INT.   CORRIDOR TO KITCHEN.   DAY.   99.

A corridor off the kitchen. Redundant bathroom and toilets.
The initial shock is over. Sorrow has matured. A FRENCH
WOMAN at the end of the corridor quietly comforts her
CAMBODIAN FAMILY. At this end ROCKOFF, SCHANBERG and DOUGAL.
Electric whispers and state of high agitation.

                    ROCKOFF
          All I need's a developer. Some
          kinds powerful sulphide. I get
          that, I can improvise the rest.

ROCKOFF is pushing the door to the kitchen. Punching his
palm with frustration.

100.   INT.   KITCHEN, CHANCELLERY, FRENCH EMBASSY.   DAY.   100.

A startling contrast to the Hall de Reception. GENDARME
and several of the lesser EMBASSY STAFF around a table
having lunch. Cold chicken and chilled wine. Plus an
abundance of frozen vegetables. Emergency generators and
water supplies make the atmosphere almost pleasant.

DOUGAL and SCHANBERG clatter in with buckets. Plastic
bottles slung round their necks. Reciprocal surprise.
The INTRUDERS can't believe the wealth of food and the
FRENCH can't believe they've been caught with it.
Uncomfortable to get nabbed with a trapful of chicken when
everyone else is starving. As usual with the FROGS they
shelter behind indignation. With an expression of contempt
DOUGAL leads the way to the sink. Fills his buckets with
bottles. Folds arms and stares at the ASSEMBLED while
SCHANBERG fills his. A punishing grin that would flatten
any appetite but a Gaul's. "Merde, alors!", from a fat
one and the jowls are back in action. SCHANBERG and
DOUGAL stagger to the door.

Halfway there and it opens. In comes another GAUL with a
GERMAN SHEPHERD. What happens now stops DOUGAL in his
tracks. The GENDARME opens a refrigerator and bungs a
steak on the floor. While the DOG gets at it he rummages
for himself. DOUGAL and his buckets traverse the room.

                    DOUGAL
          You think he'd like a little mustard
          with it? The Dog? You speak English?

6

SCENE 104.   INT. DARKROOM. DAY.   (this has been designated Sc.104 by the
                                   Script person, but is actually starting at Sc.102A, and is
                                   then intended to cut into other scenes until ROCKOFF enters
                                   Sc.98a, which is now moved later in script).

ROCKOFF and SWAIN are in the lavatory which has been blacked out.
They examine the developed negative.

ROCKOFF selects a negative. SWAIN shines his torch onto the printing
paper which has been sandwiched with the negative.
The exposed paper is put into the developer, and the image of PRAN
is slowly revealed. ROCKOFF & SWAIN are jubilant.

ROCKOFF puts the paper into the fixer as SWAIN opens the door
to tell SYD & PRAN of their progress. ROCKOFF yells to him to
shut the door.

The image slowly clouds over and fogs.

Later: a second print is being developed. It looks good. It
is transferred to the fixer as ROCKOFF & SWAIN watch.
The image in the fixer bleaches away and vanishes.

ROCKOFF has a fit of rage and asks SWAIN to leave him alone.
He starts to print again.

Later still: ROCKOFF has successfully fixed the image.

7

D.C's notes after meeting with D.P on July 31st 1983.

1. Following Sc.95, in which SWAIN tells SCHANBERG that all the Cambodians
    must leave the Embassy, play a new scene with SWAIN & ROCKOFF to start
    the passport story. Stress the importance of the need to succeed since
    without papers, PRAN is virtually a dead man.

2. Add dialogue to four-shot outside Embassy Visa section (slate 1092, al-
    ready shot), to motivate SCHANBERG's action in Sc.98.

3. Move Sc.98a to later point in script.

4. After Sc.98 cut directly to Sc.101, which tells us that ROCKOFF has a
    camera, and film, and a darkroom, but no chemicals.

5. Then to Sc.100, to keep idea of chemicals alive.

6. Now play Sc.102, then to a new scene, in which ROCKOFF manages to develop
    the negative, maybe with SWAIN's help. Now comes the tricky part (which
    DP and I did not discuss), i.e., how to Print it? My suggestion is that
    ROCKOFF digs deep into his photographic training and recalls how Daguerre
    or Fox-Talbot made their early prints, by sunlight acting on coated paper
    which would lead us directly into 'Montage country' - making the print
    combined with PRAN rehearsing his new name ... the print is blotchy or
    stained, is torn up, ROCKOFF tries again ... this time it looks good. He
    turns on the light. The image of PRAN is good, and looks as though it will
    last. Cut this onto a new version of Sc.98a in which ROCKOFF does not
    appear to have failed (not a re-shoot, just a re-cut).

7. With all the above going on, and needing to be all of a piece, we may have
    to either re-locate or cut Sc.103. Once Sc.98a is reached we should go
    directly to the passports handed in.

8. The idea of having a few cuts in which PRAN is practising his new name
    may have been dealt with in note 6, above.

9. Whilst I think of it ... the shot we have already in which SWAIN is eras-
    ing part of his name from the passport looks very botched, and no authority
    would look twice before throwing it out. Perhaps this insert should be

8

11

12

re-done? The part where the photograph is removed is OK. Maybe we
could use the 'doctoring' of the passport as part of the Montage I have
suggested in note 6?

Additional thoughts:- maybe place the interior part of Sc.103 after
the passports are handed in, and then go directly to scene 106 in
which the KR delivers the pigs. Then cut scene 107 altogether so that
we go straight to the pigs being cut up after they're delivered, and
maintain the political arguing between NOAKES & MACENTIRE. I suggest
cutting scene 107 as it is quite lengthy and is not giving us too
much required information.
After PRAN'S photograph is seen to have become invisible, suggest we
cut directly to scene 110.

David has requested a new close-shot of SWAIN to cut into scene 113.

9

96. CONTINUED:
...are American. Help us." But America has no miracles on offer. America is scared as the rest. SCHANBERG pulls away searches desperately with his eyes. Finally he gets to PRAN. Attaches himself to a GROUP that includes SAMON. Possessions are loaded into the back of a Toyota truck. Hopelessness provides a curious dignity. It is SCHANBERG who carries the horror. PRAN who tries to lighten it.

PRAN
I try to get to Thailand, Syd. Maybe two, three weeks, maybe a bit more. If you get there first leave message for me at Reuters.

SCHANBERG can't find the words. Can hardly focus what he's coping with.

SCHANBERG
Gimme an hour. Just gimme an hour will you? I need some time to think.

PRAN looks down and shakes his head. The Toyota is already on the move.

PRAN
I got no time to give ....

He turns away to join the others. SCHANBERG is an instant from tears. ROCKOFF has been running hard and breathless like he can hardly speak.

ROCKOFF
Syd. Syd. Swain's got an idea.

A balloon of hope. SARUN has already disappeared through the gate. PRAN looks at them, looks at SCHANBERG.

97. INT. RECEPTION, HALL DE RECEPTION, DAY
The RUSSIANS are eating under the stairs. Boiled eggs and vodka. Oblivious to the suffering around them. Dozens of FAMILIES unable to accept this engulfing nightmare. Dozens of desperate little schemes evolving. Anyone who isn't crying is formulating some kind of plan. And here's one of them. Urgent discussions in a corner. SCHANBERG, ROCKOFF and SWAIN. The latter has a handful of British passports. Two or three connected with blue consular ribbon. PRAN watches from the entrance. He's holding onto a rope attached to an ascending zeppelin. Let go now before it's too late? Or hang on with the horrifying fear he may loose his grip?

SCHANBERG
We think we can put a passport together ....

---

97. CONTINUED:
Hope in everyone's eyes but Pran's. He looks blankly at the documents.

SWAIN
Out of date with a current visa ... We knock out the Jon, knock out the Swain, and we get "Ankgstill Brewer".

PRAN is clearly worried by the name. Also difficulty in pronouncing it.

PRAN
Hankstill Blewer?

SWAIN
It's a bit of a mouthful, but you'll have to practise...

Everyone stares at PRAN willing him to say yes. Everyone sees a good chance in the idea. But PRAN is reluctantly forced to shake his head.

PRAN
I haven't got a picture. I never got my Identity papers back ...

98. INT. STAIRS/CORRIDOR/OFFICE, HALL DE RECEPTION, DAY
SCHANBERG takes the stairs in threes. Blind to the crush of anguish. Races along a corridor. Checks several offices converted into dormitories. Finally finds what he's looking for. This room has been adapted into a clinic. Stomach complaints. At least one case of dysentery. The NURSES wipe everything down with strong solution of disinfectant. SUNDSVALL kneels on the damp floors administering to a CHILD.

SCHANBERG
You got a Polaroid camera?

SUNDSVALL removes his stethoscope. Almost as distracted as SCHANBERG.

SUNDSVALL
Yes.

Returns attention to his PATIENT annihilating an instant of elation.

SUNDSVALL
But I have no film. I have no metronidazole. The child has dysentery.

One horror is absorbed by another. SCHANBERG has already disappeared.

98"A". INT. KITCHEN, HALL DE RECEPTION, DAY
DOUGAL sits at a table making glue with cooked rice. PRAN sits opposite with his head in his hands. "My name is Hank-at-ill Blewer." He emanates a despair infecting everybody. A kettle steams behind him. SCHANBERG and SWAIN carefully peel out the written section of the passport. Everyone is aware that everything is useless without a photograph.

The last hope of it arrives in the door. Everybody except PRAN looks at ROCKOFF. He shakes his head. The atmosphere implodes. PRAN senses it and looks up. His expression is so sad and desperate it is almost like love. ROCKOFF is unable to tell him the truth.

ROCKOFF
Well. There you go. We're in luck.

PRAN's eyes light up like a child's and tears spill down his face.

PRAN
Oh. Ai. Thank you Al.

3   4   5

(1–13) **The Killing Fields**: Notes from a meeting Jim had with David Puttnam following the decision to rewrite an area of the film (8–9). "Often there is the need for retakes and rethinking after a rough cut has revealed a story flaw – Puttnam always built retakes into the budget. On **The Killing Fields** we had several additional shoots." Marked up script for scenes relating to the memo (1–7).

111

jim clark

13

– such as a good line reading or a certain look, regardless of whether the director has asked me to use that take or not. After this I will start actual editing, building up the scene cut by cut without attempting to refine it. I leave in sound overlaps, bad matches and other obvious mistakes, whilst trying to use the best material. After a second pass I save the scene, copy it and start again, this time looking at all the out-takes as I go; eventually I may have several versions of the same scene. Finally I will take a bit from one version and a section from another, thus making up a final version. When I feel I have a good shape, which can take many passes and many days, I decide what music should accompany the scene. The music that I impose on the film in the early stages can be important: if everyone agrees the mood and tone of the temp music is fitting, it generally remains on the film throughout previews. Then the composer (poor fellow) is often confronted by a *fait accompli* unless he is able to come up with a different composition which works equally well. In any case, once a scene begins to take shape, I then start refining the sound, which is a far more complex job than it used to be. When working on magnetic film the editor was required to attend to the sound in a more rudimentary way. Now we spend as much time refining sound as we spend on the action – for a start there are unlimited tracks at our command and fitting sound from other takes, or cutting wild tracks is a very quick and easy procedure on an AVID or Lightworks.

When you get down to cutting how do you know if a cut is good? Well, most people would say "a cut which is unnoticeable is good." The old adage is that if you start looking at the editing, the film has not got your full attention. It is true that if I find myself outside the film I may pay attention to the editing style. Some films fail to involve me because the editing is paying too much attention to itself. I'm thinking of films where editorial flourish often stands in for lack of substance – one looks in amazement and wonders just why certain scenes have emerged in such a fractured way and what does it mean? However, in any case, there are surely no rules as such. One tries to make a scene as smooth as possible, cut for cut, in order to keep the story flowing – movements should be matched for this reason – continuity should be maintained whenever possible. Dead footage should be avoided. Pauses, sometimes essential, can also be irksome.

Ralph Sheldon, a fellow editor, is credited with making a remark which is often quoted to directors: "no matter how you cut it, it's still salami!". I have quoted this astute but unkind remark on numerous occasions and sometimes without offence. It really reflects those films that have been cut, re-cut and re-cut again, countless times, without ever really coming to the boil. There is a moment when every film finds its construction and its length, and one should recognise that moment.

The great glory of digital editing, and one of its strengths, is that it is very forgiving! An editor can make a mess of a scene and trash it; but thereby hangs one of the worst aspects of the machine. It can be too forgiving. There are plenty of examples around where digital editing has resulted in a rapid-fire meaningless mess which often passes for "creative" editing

1

2

3

Jim had been asked to prepare a 30-minute product reel of **The Killing Fields** for Warner Bros. and Far Eastern distributors. The notes reveal that he prepared a short script for Puttnam's approval (4–5). "We do quite a lot of promotional material as well as the feature. There is always a demand for extracts that get shown at trade conventions, or for companies who have product placement. On **The World is Not Enough** (3) we cut several teaser trailers though MGM finally cut their own trailer." (1–2) "I always mark up my own script from the rushes. If there is a huge collection of shots, I put them into a database to access them more easily. I started this when cutting **Memphis Belle**. I had many takes of planes doing a variety of manoeuvres (B17s, Messerschmits etc.) and a database allowed me to organise them."

To: David Puttnam
From: Jim Clark

September 21st 1983

KILLING FIELDS Promotional reel

Following our talk the other day, I have written out a simple structure script for this product reel, including some titles which I shall have made if you agree.

The reel will open with the words "Selected Scenes from ..." superimposed over a red background. The "Killing Fields" logo zooms into this shot as it did on the front of our original product reel, and fades out to black as the following words roll out -

Opening text (version 1)

In 1973, Sydney Schanberg, working for the New York Times, became their correspondent in Cambodia. Throughout his passed shame he was assisted by a local man, Dith Pran. THE KILLING FIELDS tells the story of their relationship and of Dith Pran's eventual fate in the hands of the Khmer Rouge.

Opening text (version 2)

"I began the search for my friend Dith Pran in April 1975. Unable to protect him when the Khmer Rouge troops ordered Cambodians to evacuate their cities, I had watched him disappear into the interior of Cambodia, which would become a death camp for millions.....

(at this point, fade in a still of PRAN and cover rest of text onscreen)

... Dith Pran had saved my life the day of the occupation, and the shadow of my failure to keep him safe was to follow me for four and a half years.

This is a story of war and friendship, of the anguish of a ruined country and of one man's will to live."

Sydney Schanberg.

(Unfreeze C.S. of PRAN as roller clears - PRAN smiles).

If you think that either version of the text is wrong, or too long-winded, please let me know - or rewrite it as you would like it.

4

Whether we use an opening text or not, I would suggest superimposing a title on the start of the shot in which Sydney opens the window at Neak Lung - :-

CAMBODIA 1973

to let the folks know where we are.

After this we will have the whole of the Neak sequence as cut presently, followed by part of the Press conference, maybe playing part of it over some other shots (I was thinking of some refugee shots, or some of the wounded people), and then leading into the Coca-Cola sequence followed by the Embassy party, reduced to the opening scene with the Ambassador, through Reeves singing, then to Reeves talking to Rockoff which goes directly to Auld Lang Syne - in abbreviated form. After this, go to Scene 47, also shortened, and then to the Liberation of the City (over which I would put another title:- PHOM PENH 1975). Then the Arrest sequence and the Evacuation. Use a title to introduce the French Embassy, see the people arriving over the fence, and then use the scene where Swain tells Sydney that the Cambodians have to leave, followed by part of the scene with Rockoff and Swain which tells you that Pran will be dead if he leaves the Embassy. After this play the whole piece of Pran's departure.

Maybe here we should insert another title, on black, which tells you that Schanberg returned to New York as Pran was sent to the fields by the Khmer Rouge?

Now see Pran in the fields with the other toilers, and show some other shots of him in the camp, ending with his escape and the Skulls.

End with Schanberg and Pran reunited and perhaps freeze the final frame as they embrace, bringing up the John Lennon song (which I will try and use earlier if possible).

I shall cut this together as indicated,(unless you think of any alternative way to do it) on a black & white dupe, and show it to you on Oct 5th as arranged. I will dub it after you have seen it and I've made changes - unless you feel you will not be able to judge it unmixed. Please give me an answer on this so that I can make arrangements to book the dubbing theatre. We will have colour reprints made only after you have passed the reel.

Jim Clark

P.S. Would we need a further title at the end to tell the audience when the film/book will be available? or any other credits?

c.c. Roland Joffé
     Iain Smith

5

"For the scene in **Marathon Man** when Babe's (Dustin Hoffman) apartment is entered whilst he is in the bath (1–2), we required that he should react on hearing whispered voices off-screen. No actual words were to be heard. For screenings my assistant, Artie Schmidt, and I recorded these voices for the temp track – and they never left the film. I guess we did something right! When Babe is being tortured by the dentist's drill very little is actually shown (3–4). It is a powerful scene whilst not being visually explicit. Most of us are nervous in the hands of the dentist so the sequence carries a lot of anxiety from the audience, therefore it was not necessary to actually show the drill going into Babe's teeth. The sound effect of the drill was crucial to the effect we desired. As the drill came closer and began to go out of focus we altered the pitch of the drill, as if it were boring into something hard. The sound continued until the camera panned to the white light when the drill stops and Babe's scream is heard. The out-of-focus image was created in the optical printer, as was the zoom into the white light."

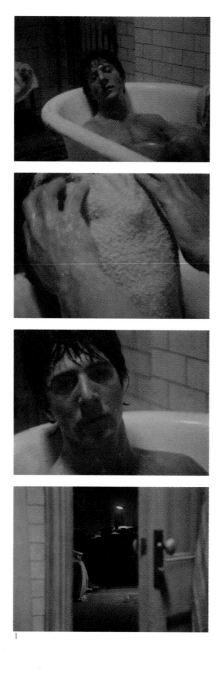

1

2

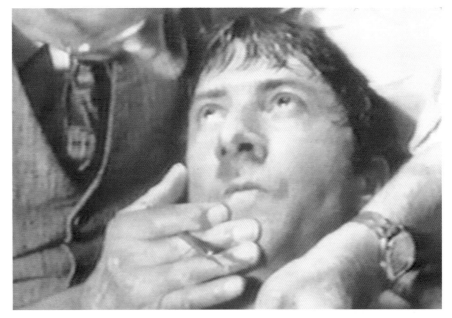

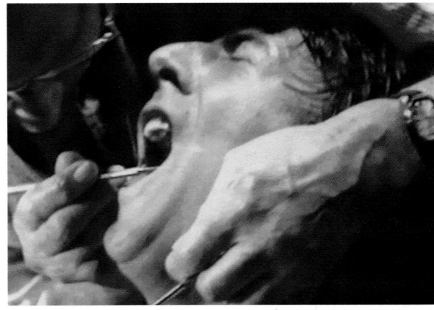

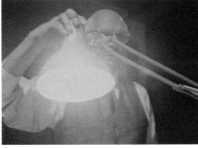

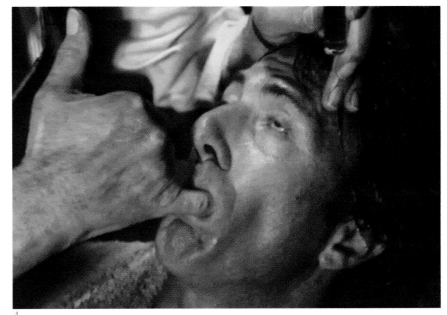

3

4

(1) "One trick I use occasionally within a scene is to skip print (only print every other frame) in order to remove half a pause. This optical device was especially useful when I was re-cutting **Twilight**, since Paul Newman was given to long pauses resulting in dead footage. I was able to help him out from time to time with my skip-printing trick. Of course this only works if there is no fast movement within the section." (2) "Sometimes directors have a bad time with an actor and then do everything they can to wreck the performance in the cutting room out of sheer spite. I recall Michael Caton-Jones developed a vendetta against Ellen Barkin when making **This Boy's Life**, in which she played the mother. He ruthlessly cut her material and, when she was on-screen he would cut away from her and play her dialogue while we see another character whenever possible – directors can get their own back this way. Schlesinger, when experiencing problems with actors would say 'don't forget, we have the scissors!'." (3) "In the cutting room a performance can be made or marred. Jack Harris, the editor of **The Prince and the Showgirl** – on which Jim was assistant – had many problems with Marilyn Monroe's inability to match movements (she was very short-sighted) and would massage the cuts for hours in order to achieve the smoothest edit. He referred to it as 'love cutting' – that is where you are doing your darndest to help the actor out of a hole."

and is liable to impress the viewer with its flash and dazzle, whether it helps the story or not. This "anything goes" or "blender" approach owes a lot to the music video (which, in my view, has nothing in common with the feature film). So there are editors working who do not fully deserve the title – it is just too plain easy to use an AVID and call yourself an editor. In times past, the editor was forced to think about what he was doing. Formerly, before the advent of the Italian splicer (anyone under 30 will not remember it) the editor would lose two frames every time he altered a cut. These two frames then had to be built up with black spacing in order to keep sync. This called for discipline and one could tell the confident editor by the number of black frames featured in his cut. The modern way does not display this indecision. It does not help to sort out the men from the boys or the good from the merely competent. Jack Harris, one of the most brilliant editors of his day, would survey his rushes on a spool-loading Moviola, running the material back and forth for sometimes days before he would commit himself. The moment his scissors cut the film, however, was supreme – he had the scene assembled in his head and from then on he rarely changed anything. There were very few black frames in his cutting copy! Of course one has to recall that editors in those days did not have the plethora of material which is commonplace today with multi-camera set-ups giving rise to many possibilities. They had minimal cover and far fewer printed takes – so in many ways it was an easier task.

For all this work done by an editor, one tends to forget in the fastness of the cutting room that other hands have already shaped the material you handle. The clay, so to speak, has already been dragged into submission by many other people. Our task as editors is to take the clay and produce the most satisfactory pot, which the director might then be happy to call his own, put on his mantelpiece and say "I made that!". Other potters will then survey and assess this piece and remark upon it. Although the film director is playing with more expensive materials the act of creation is much the same.

Dede Allen was born in 1924. She started out in the film industry at the age of 18 with a job as a messenger with Columbia, from here she moved into the sound editing department for three years. Following a period as an assistant in the picture department, Dede went to New York where she cut commercials and industrials. Her second feature was **Odds Against Tomorrow** (1959), directed by Robert Wise

dede allen

who had cut for Orson Welles. It was a nerve-wracking experience for the novice editor. "In those days we had 'hot splices' and every time you made a cut you had to put a black slug in, because you lost a frame with every splice. I was very nervous because this meant Robert Wise could see every time I had reworked the first scene I showed him. But he said: 'Good girl, I see you're not afraid to work with it until it plays – I like that.' He was a wonderful inspiration and gave me my confidence." Since then Dede has gone on to work for directors such as Robert Rossen (**The Hustler**, 1961), Elia Kazan (**America, America**, 1963), Arthur Penn (**Bonnie and Clyde,** 1967), Sidney Lumet (**Serpico**, 1973) and many more. In 1992 she became head of post-production at Warner Brothers, returning to the cutting room to cut **Wonder Boys** (2000, Curtis Hanson), for which she received an Oscar nomination. As well as being celebrated for her editing, Dede Allen is also famous for training up many of America's biggest editors who worked as assistants in her cutting rooms.

As a film editor, you have to know what the scene is and where the performances are. Ironically the best way to learn what makes a scene or a performance, is by watching live theatre rather than movies, because everything you see in movies has been put together after the event. When you are watching a play you can see the actors improvise and observe where the performance is and where the scene is. Of course theatre performance is different from what you do in movies, but fundamentally acting for the stage and acting for the camera are both about making a scene work. So I always advise people to go and see plays. I like the theatre experience. I was very lucky because I had a lot of theatre training when I started in film. My mother had been a stage actress until she met my father, and my grandfather loved the theatre. He was actually very surprised when I wanted to get involved with movies because for him theatre was what it was all about, however, I had become a big movie buff. I began as a messenger in the sound department of Columbia. At the

120

1

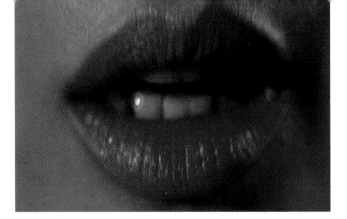

2

(1–2) "The opening titles on **Bonnie and Clyde** were wonderful, featuring actual photos of families in the mid-West. When Jack Warner first saw them he was furious. I found Warren saying to Wayne, the title man: 'You are fantastic but I beg you – never take something we have worked on and show it to the studio first.' But of course they always need to show them to the studio first."

same time I was working every evening in the Actors Lab, which was a wonderful place full of marvellous actors who had come from the Group Theatre in New York. I spent five years working there as I moved from messenger to apprentice, and then started as a sound editor. All the time I was learning about theatre, lights, props, direction and performance. It was a wonderful training ground. Now as a picture editor, when I cut, I'm thinking about character and story. When I start to cut a scene I organise it by breaking it up into its beats – beat one, beat two, beat three. That is what a scene is made up of – moments of drama. It could be a short scene made up of one or two beats. If it is a long scene with six beats, I divide it up into the six beats and I work on the sections, cutting it in continuity. For example, if you have a scene with three people talking you look at what they are talking about; the first beat is about one thing and then the conversation changes and goes on to the next subject or beat, and then it will change again and so on. Basically I am dividing up the scene in a way that I can memorise it more easily and which relates to the drama. Beats are really a term out of theatre training; directors who come out of the theatre talk in beats.

The rhythm in which a scene is played is dictated by the actors, but it is also dictated by the editor. The editor has to make the performance. You cannot just let things play exactly the way they were in reality. Sometimes you have to energise a scene, shrinking time and pacing shots – pacing is a very important factor in how you put it together. Then you begin developing the characters. Sometimes a character will do one thing three different times in three different scenes, so you have to take that out because it's happening in other scenes. This is all part of the cutting down process when you begin to pace up the film. As an editor, you must be aware of what the scene is, what the character is doing and importantly whom you have as an actor. What the editor moulds is a result of the writing (since nothing happens without the writing), and then the direction, but also the actors who work the material and very often change it. For example, the script of **Dog Day Afternoon** had the potential to be extremely camp. It could have been absolutely tasteless with the fat wife and the transvestites. It would not have worked if there was no sympathy for the characters, so it was very important how it was cast. At one point, Sidney was considering real transvestites who could not act and it was campy which meant you did not have any sympathy. So he decided to cast an actor and that is when Chris Sarandon got the part. On the other hand, in **Wonder Boys** there is a transvestite who plays Antonia/Tony who has never acted in a movie before and he is wonderful. So you do not have to be a fully trained actor.

All actors are different, some are highly trained theatrically, others totally intuitive. I've worked with great actors who are very inventive and aren't always the same in every take. This gives the editor more choice but you must also be careful to maintain consistency. Sometimes even good actors will have quirks which you have to get around and cut out – like blinking or smacking teeth together. Every performer has certain personal idiosyncrasies and sometimes that is great, they could be idiosyncrasies that they have worked hard to develop and which are part of either the character or their star

(1) When Bonnie goes to meet her mother in a quarry in **Bonnie and Clyde**, the scene is presented in such a way that we sense that death is just around the corner. "The visuals were shot with different filters and were all matched in post-production by using an optical neg – a trick I knew from my days working in commercials. We made some of it so you cannot hear it, more distant conversations are going on in various places and you hear the wind blowing paper away – it all made up a style developed for that scene." (2) "I approach dailies in a gut instinct way – I am driven by the performance. I sit next to the director and make notes. (3) Elia Kazan did not want me to take my eyes off the screen on **America, America**. I had a great big book and I would just write from left to right as he went along, so I had the notes and they were legible to a degree! Each director is different, sometimes you get notes, sometimes you get grunts, sometimes you get nothing!"

"On **Dog Day Afternoon** the scene outside the bank between Durning and Pacino was improvised (2). Lumet had a camera run on each of them and I cut it together using pieces from each – keeping it going so that they were talking over each other. The phone conversation between Pacino and the transvestite, played by Chris Sarandon, (1) was done just as two or three takes on each character with a lot of improvisation and it worked very well."

quality personality. In this case you use the idiosyncrasies, because that is what you are selling as a star. But normally you can improve performances by cleaning out these tics. You protect the scene, the performance, the actor, and the character by just getting what's best out of a performer. So sometimes you have to cut away for the wrong reasons. If an actor blows a line, you have to go to someone else, but usually I try to cut to someone else for a reason. It still has to look smooth, it cannot look as though you are weaving the performance, it has to look as though it's logical. This can be very difficult. Some people cannot judge editing unless it is flashy and flashy editing is the easiest thing to do. Montages and fights are much easier than a conversation around a table, especially if you have any weak actors.

For example, **The Breakfast Club** is basically talking heads – in this case a group of high-school kids during a day in detention – and the job of the editor is to keep the talking heads moving. The head of the studio at the time did not like the picture – he kept calling it the group therapy session! When an editor has a group of characters chatting among themselves you have to know at what point to cut to someone else. For me it is all a matter of feeling. I know who the characters are and what they are doing in a particular scene. In **The Breakfast Club** what each character was doing was so important. Ally Sheedy had a part in which she hardly spoke, but it was still a very important role. You had to know when to cut to her even though she did not speak! It is a difficult job, but when it works, as one of my assistants said to me: "You make the film dance!" The irony is that a very good

about three or four Academy Awards said to me: "Oh, I couldn't figure out why you took that odd picture. I thought it was so cute, but it was so simple." It wasn't simple at all – it was a very difficult picture to cut. I figured, well if this guy doesn't understand, nobody will! It was all dialogue so you had to keep it going and make it appeal to an audience.

The Breakfast Club was shot on location so there was unwanted background noise that made some of the dialogue hard to hear. We had to bring the actors back to re-record the unclear lines. This is called ADR, or looping, and happens in almost every feature film. An actor is brought to a studio and you project the section with the bad sound again and again until the actor can match the lips on the screen with a new recording which is in sync with the original recording from the shoot. I always get upset with someone who says they will not loop. Altman is a very good example of it. A couple of Altman's pictures drove me crazy in the beginning. He is a wonderful man and a great director, but at this time he did not believe in looping. He felt he would not get the original performance. Other directors actually want to loop, even if you can hear the recorded line perfectly, because they want a new line reading that will change a performance. On one film this particular actress suddenly began realising how she could improve her performance by re-recording most of her dialogue. She got away with doing it and ended up with an Academy Award nomination! I make sure a scene follows a rhythm. Sometimes I prefer to stay in a master longer, but then a director will come in and say no I want to see the close-ups so you do it in the close-ups. I do not have any

editing & post-production

1

(1) The fast cutting in **Bonnie and Clyde** was later imitated. The killing of Bonnie and Clyde contained 51 shots in 54 seconds. "Some people cannot judge editing unless it is flashy, but flashy editing is the easiest thing to do... easier than a conversation around a table."

close-ups so you do it in the close-ups. I do not have any rules. I remember when I started at Columbia there were some very sweet editors who would take me aside and teach me. There was one guy who was a very nice man. He said, "You always start with a master and then you move in to this shot, and then you move in to that shot, and then you go to the close-up." Well you don't do that. I sometimes start with a close-up, it just depends! Directing, and therefore editing, has taken a totally different form. If you look at an old movie you see people stay in a two shot for a long time. It was a budget issue, the cameras did not have the fluidity, people did not have these hand-held cameras, or those little wonderful dollies that were later developed where you can zip in and out. In the early days they did not shoot as much footage. So there were not a million ways to put it together.

Of course there are rules in editing, there are all kinds of rules you have to know and then you can break them. I have broken them all! In a nutshell, a good cut is when you do not see it unless you want to. The whole idea is that you should be watching the drama unfold as if it were something that is happening and not be distracted by the editing. Then sometimes you draw attention to the cutting if it is a style. **Bonnie and Clyde** definitely changed the cutting style in features, because people began to imitate it by going faster. The early cuts of the film were very loose. Towards the end Arthur Penn was just saying: "Go through it again, go through it again and cut it down." He wanted the movie to move – it was a very desperate time and a desperate kind of story about people on the run. There were people in Hollywood who considered **Bonnie and Clyde** the worst cut picture they had ever seen. I did not get nominated for an Academy Award for that picture at all. Then they began to imitate it and it became a whole different style. We faded out one scene and cut in the following scene – rather than the accepted practice of fading out and then fading in. When we showed it to Jack Warner, who was the head of the studio, he said, "You mean you're going to fade out and cut in?" and Arthur said "Yes, that's what we're going to do." Warner thought it was the worst picture he had ever seen. He never understood the success of that picture. We would never have been able to finish the film the way we did if there had not been a six-day war in Israel and Warner was getting ready to leave the studio! And, of course producer Warren Beatty's persistence won the day.

Nowadays it is the young audience in the malls who control what you are seeing because this is the audience that the studio previews your film to. It is through such previews that the studio decides how much money they are going to put in for publicity and how much money they are going to put towards finishing the movie – and what previews well in malls are often these dumb action pictures or fast dumb comedies. So now we are in the age of massive sound and action. However, when you get a movie with just stories and scenes, people also like to see that, because such a picture has got much more meat in it. When the picture you are working on has a theatrical release it will reach thousands of people – that is why it is a shame if it is not good.

"In **The Breakfast Club**, (1–2) a movie of 'talking heads' rather than action, the difficulty was keeping all the characters 'alive'."

biography

Pietro Scalia was born in Sicily, Italy in 1960. He grew up admiring the great American movies of Stanley Donen, John Ford and Howard Hawks. "Later as a teenager I was exposed to Italian movies. I loved how raw they were in their emotions." He discovered the art of editing during his years as a film student at UCLA. Pietro started as an assistant editor on Konchalovsky's **Shy People** in 1987. Konchalovsky

pietro scalia

wanted to cut the film himself which gave Pietro the opportunity to act as his pair of hands and thereby learn more about editing. He set his sights on working with Oliver Stone and begged a friend to introduce him to Stone's editor, Claire Simpson. He managed to get a job as assistant to Claire on **Wall Street** (1987) and then as assistant to David Brenner on **Talk Radio** (1988). He went on to get an associate editor credit on **Born on the Fourth of July** (1989) and an additional editor position on **The Doors** (1991). This led to a chief editor position on **JFK** (1991) along with Joe Hutching. Pietro has since worked with Bernardo Bertolucci (**Little Buddha**, 1993; **Stealing Beauty**, 1995), Sam Raimi (**The Quick and the Dead**, 1995), Gus Van Sant (**Good Will Hunting**, 1997) and Ridley Scott (**Gladiator**, 2000 – for which he received the BAFTA – and **Hannibal**, 2001).

interview

I fell in love with the art of editing during my years as a film student at UCLA. There I felt the power of editing. I could see how you could manipulate the images. I spent months at film school in a dark room working on an old Moviola editing machine, rediscovering the material that was shot by the other students. I realised the excitement of being able to rewrite with images by changing their context and creating a new emotional response. Really the job of the editor is the job of a storyteller. He is also the sculptor or architect – somebody who will take all the raw materials provided and put them together as a cohesive whole. He must create something that makes sense, something built around the story and with characters that affect the viewer in an emotional way.

However, before you really begin to build the (hopefully) aesthetically pleasing structure, you must start with the technical basics. Normally the editor will begin about a week before the production starts to shoot. You set up a cutting

1

2

3

editing & post-production

In **Good Will Hunting**, Pietro "tended to go for the early takes from Robin Williams (1) where he was low-key. As the takes progressed he became more artificial, more exaggerated. When Robin Williams saw the film, he was shocked because it seemed far from the performance he thought he had delivered!" The final scene order in the film (4) was changed from the original script order. "We had to get to the dramatic elements at the start more quickly so we moved things around. The position of the girl leaving Will was too early (2). We repositioned her character at strategic points throughout the story so that by the end she would be more meaningful to Will. This was at the expense of Will's friendship with the Ben Affleck character (3). However, I think that by strengthening the love interest, we made it more interesting. I had an earful from Ben Affleck though, who was also one of the scriptwriters!"

GOOD WILL HUNTING CONTINUITY

CUT 7   A/O 10/06/97

FOOTAGE   START = 0

Reel	Sc	Description	Min/Sec	Length
1AB C7	1-3C	Title Sequence - Prism Montage / Will reading/ Chuckie picks up Will		
	4	Int. MIT Classroom - Lambeau offers fame in MIT Math review		
	5D	Int. MIT Hallway - Will mops floor + sees problem on blackboard		
	59	Int. L St. Bar - Kathy makes fun of Chuckie @ bar		
	16A/95	Int. Will's Apt - Will does math on mirror/rides subway		
	16B	Int. MIT Hallway - Will shines floor and does math		
	5	Int. Batting Cage - Chuckie tells about party @ Harvard bar		
	7	Ext. MIT Campus - M.I.T. Reunion		
	9	Int. MIT Hallway - Lambeau discovers problem solved		
	8	Ext. Park - Boys @ Little League Game		
	10	Int. Chuckie's Car - Boys talk about Double Burger		
	11-13	Ext. Basketball Court - Fight/Will is arrested		
	17	Ext. MIT Campus - Students stream to one class in particular		
	18	Int. MIT Classroom - Math Magician refuses to step forward		
	16	Ext. Courthouse - Chuckie picks up Will		
	20	Int. MIT Hallway - Lambeau finds Will solving problem		
	21	Ext. Pub - Will tells boys he has been fired		
	22-23	Int. Pub - Will defends Chuckie	1820+09	20:06
2AB C7	24	Int. Pub - Skylar meets Will		
	25	Ext. Pub - Will tells Clark he's got Skylar's number		
	26-26C	Int. Night Boston/Will's Apt. - Chuckie drops off Will		
	27	Int. MIT Bldg/Grnd Garage - Lambeau looks for Will		
	28	Int. Courtroom - Will defends himself/Lambeau comes in		
	29-29A	Int. County Jail Hallway-Will calls Skylar		
	30	Int. Interrogation Room-Lambeau tells Will conditions of release		
	59A	Int. Lambeau office - Will and Lambeau collaborate on math problem		
	32	Int. Wills apartment-Will speed reads Lipkins book		
	33	Int. Psychologists office-Will analyses the analyst		
	34	Int. Hallway-Lipkins doesn't have time for pro-bono		
	37	Int. Hypnotists Office-Will sings "Skyrockets" for Hypno.		
	44	Ext. Bunker Hill Campus-Establish Campus		
	38	Int. Bunker Hill Campus-Sean teaches Psychology class		
	41	Int. Lockober Restaurant - Sean & Lambeau talk about reunion		
	31	Int. Funland-Will tells Chuckie about probation and therapy		
	43	Int. Lockober Restaurant-Lambeau convinces Sean to counsel Will		
	45	Int. Seans office-1" counseling session with Sean / painting analysis	1974+03	21:49
3AB C7	46-47	Int. Seans office -Will leaves/Sean agrees to continue with Will		
	49	Int. Seans Apt -Sean is deep in thought		
	40	Int. Toy Store-Will & Skylar first date		
	42	Int. Tasty-Will and Skylar have first kiss		
	50	Int. Seans Office-Sean tells Will to follow		
	51	Ext. Boston Common-Sean tells Will as it's "his call"		
	57	Ext. Wills Apt.-Chuckie picks up Will		
	52	Int. Construction Site-Will and Chuckie do Demo		
	53-53A	Ext.Boston Street-Will calls Skylar and Hangs up		
	54	Int. Seans Office-Will counting seconds in silence		
	55	Int. Hallway-Sean tells Lambeau he won't talk first		
	65	Int. Lambeau's Office - Will changed Alexander's theory		
	60	Int. Seans Office-Will tells Sean about Skylar/Sean talks about his wife		
	60AA- 61	Ext. Skylars Dorm - She has O-Chem/no time for date		
	62	Ext. Harvard Sq. - Will solves O-Chem		
	62A-63	Ext. Skylars Dorm-Will can not wait until tomorrow for a date		
	48	Ext. Wonderland Dog Race -Will lies about his big family	1911+09	21:07
4AB C7V2	64	Int. Seans Office/ "Pudge Fisk"- Sean tells Will how he met his wife		
	66	Int. Skylars Dorm-Skylar & Will lovemaking and Skylar wishes to meet Will's friends		
	67	Int. L St.-Skylar swaps jokes with Chuckie, Bill and Morgan		
	68	Ext. L St.-Chuckie lends car to Will		
	70	Int. Timmys Tap-Lambeau and Sean talk about Will		
	71	Int. Tri-Tech-Chuckie poses as Will and asks for a retainer		
	72	Ext. Au Bon Pain-Skylar asks Will about his photo memory		
	76 pt	Int. Skylars Dorm-CU Will "Are you awake?"	1790+09	19:46
5AB C7V2	76	Int. Skylar's Dorm-Will tells Skylar he doesn't love her		
	75	Int. Lambeau Office-Lambeau wishes he had never met Will		
	78	Int. Chuckies House-Morgan watches porno flicks		
	77	Int. NSA Office-Why shouldn't Will work for NSA		
	85	Int. Seans Office-Sean kicks Will out for not answering		
	79-79A	Ext. S. Boston phone-Will says good-bye to Skylar		
	103	Ext. Bank of Charles River - Will thinks about Skylar		
	81/83	Int. Logan Airport-Skylar looks for Will/Plane takes off		
	86	Int. Construction Site-Will vents rage at demo job		
	87	Int. Seans Office-Will fails to show for session with Lambeau		
	89	Ext. Construction Site Parking-Will owes it to Chuckie to leave	1894+01	20:56
6AB C7	90	Int. Sean's Office - Lambeau & Sean fight/Will comes in		
	92-94	Int. Sean's Office - Sean & Will discuss childhood beatings		
	95-95B	Int. Train/Int. Will's Apt/Ext. S Boston Park - Will thinking		
	95C-96	Int. McNeil Lab - Will goes for interview		
	100	Int. Sean's Office - Will & Sean say Good-bye		
	98-99	Int./Ext. L Street Bar - Boys say Happy Birthday to Will and give Will a Chevy Nova		
	102	Int. Sean's Office - Sean & Lambeau make peace and go for a drink		
	105-116	Final Sequence - Will leaves note for Sean/Chuckie discovers Will has left		
	117	Ext. Highway - Will drives to California	1993+10	22:02
		END CRAWL		

TOTAL FOOTAGE 11384+09

TOTAL FOOTAGE W/OUT LEADERS 11312+09

TOTAL RUNNING TIME 2:05:41

GOOD WILL HUNTING

4

room on location, hire the crew and make sure that the editing equipment is organised. Once shooting begins, the shot film (or negative) is sent off to the lab every night. It is processed and comes back to the cutting room the following day. My assistants then prepare the film for a dailies screening that night, when it will be shown to the director. They sync the sound with the picture as well as log and code the film. They also prepare my screening notes which I take to the dailies screening where I make notes on what I see and any comments that the director may have.

It is exciting going to dailies. I look for things that register something with me. Why do you react differently to one take than to another? What is it about the camera movement or performance of an actor? I visually memorise the material and then I jot down some notes. I will note the size of the shot, what has changed from one take to the next and I'll incorporate whatever the director says. Obviously I'll make technical notes about whether or not the shot is in focus because this is hard to judge on the digital computer image that I will be cutting on. I look for the performance that rings true. I suppose what I really do is look for whatever appears to be truthful to me. If I can pinpoint something that affected me emotionally about the take – whether it be the performance, the shot or the composition – I will use that when I later build the scene and try to give it back to the viewer.

For example in **Stealing Beauty** there was a scene where Sinead Cusack goes and kisses her screen husband Donal McCann who is lying in bed. On the first take Donal puts his hand round her head as if to hold on to the kiss, but she disappears leaving him staring at his hand. It was a complete accident. Bertolucci liked the gesture and got them to repeat it in the subsequent takes, fine-tuning the performance and the position of the hand. However, when we projected dailies I said to Bernardo that the first take was the best. He disagreed. But I said that the first take was the best because it was real, it was not thought out. We went for the first. If you look closely you find bits where a great performance is not acted, when it is actually felt. At dailies you are trying to pick out those true bits of a film. After dailies my assistants organise the material, telecine the film on to videotape and digitise it on to my computer. Then I can start editing the scene.

Fundamentally when editing you are taking one image and putting another image right next to it. By joining these two images together you are creating meaning. For example, you can have an image of an empty glass of milk cut with an image of a man. Your brain automatically makes an association between the two and you create a new meaning: the glass of milk is now a glass of milk that the man has drunk; or the man is now a satisfied man after having drunk his milk. The actual cut has created this new meaning and the relation between the two images. Then you continue – you create another new meaning with the third image and this becomes associated with the rest of the images. It is a continuous process. It was exactly this power of editing that made **JFK** so controversial. We used the exact same visuals that the Warren Commission had used to discuss Kennedy's

1

2

3

The Zapruder film of Kennedy's assassination was integral to **JFK** (1). "Oliver said: 'the only thing I want people to remember when they walk out of this movie is the Zapruder film and to remember back and to the left' (which was the way Kennedy's head moved when he was shot). The first cut of the film was 3 hours 47 minutes long and we had to cut out 40 minutes. To not lose sense, I kept in mind that the thread of the film was always the actual assassination, the Zapruder film."

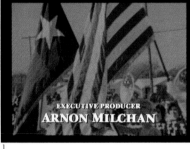

In the opening sequence of **JFK**, archive footage was cut together to create new meaning (1). Archive material was also inter-cut with material Oliver Stone had shot with actors so that it could be played back on televisions people are seen to be watching during the film (3). After fighting with his wife, Oswald goes and rents a room where he is lying on the bed, bored. "It would have been enough just to show just one shot, but we cut two shots – in one he's laying down and in the other he's sitting on the side of the bed. We did that for rhythm (the two shots rhythmically work better than just one) and for pure pleasure, for pure editing pleasure." (2)

assassination. However, when we used them they had a different meaning. The visual itself was exactly the same visual, but when you edit it into a different context within a scene it creates something new.

We used a lot of these archive visuals in the title sequence of **JFK**. This title sequence shows Kennedy arriving in Dallas, getting off the plane and going downtown through the streets of Dallas. I cut this together from stock footage that had actually been shot on the day. It was important to me to show how Kennedy was well-liked by the crowds and how much they adored him. So for example, there's one shot where Kennedy passes by in the motorcade and he looks straight into the camera of whoever was shooting that particular stock footage. I also saw a completely separate shot of a woman holding a child, also looking straight into the camera. I cut those two shots together. The cut created a connection of the eyes between Kennedy (looking straight into the camera) and the woman and child (looking straight into the camera). And at the same time I created a connection between Kennedy and the audience – who he is also looking at. Now that's completely found, it does not exist in real life, however, by cutting together those found pieces I created a meaning that's correct for the story. Kennedy was well-liked, they adored him. There was a connection between him, the woman and child, and I fabricated the connection. Most of all, there is a connection with the viewer. You have the viewer on the outside looking at Kennedy and Kennedy looking back at the viewer on the outside.

This stock footage and news reel material was acquired in **JFK** to be incorporated as news footage that would be playing on a TV monitor in somebody's house, in a bar, or in a restaurant during scenes in the film. This real archive footage would have to be inter-cut with the actors that were playing the actual historical characters in the film. For example, Oliver Stone would have to shoot Gary Oldman acting Oswald in the basement of the Dallas Police Station. We would then inter-cut that material with some of the real stock footage shot in the basement of the Dallas Police Station. Then I would cut it, replacing the real Lee Harvey Oswald with the actor Gary Oldman. This new sequence would then be put out to tape so that it could be played on a TV that somebody in the film is watching at home.

JFK is a powerful example of how the editor can create something new from previously unrelated material. On **JFK** we were criticised for distorting historical truth by taking an historical image and inter-cutting it with fictional material shot by Oliver using actors. Although we did use the same historical image, I do not think that we were distorting it. We were not trying to rewrite history, rather we were trying to make a political point, regardless of however wrong that point may be. It's very manipulative but is it amoral to a story point of view? No it isn't because I think that we're there for entertainment purposes.

However, the inter-cutting of archive with fiction did not just cause moral problems. We had 27 of these types of play-backs – a logistical nightmare! We knew that after the shoot a lot of this stock material would be very useful to incorporate within the body of the film. This would match the way Oliver shot with Bob Richardson (the cinematographer) – using and mixing various formats of film: black and white, 16mm, Super 8, 8mm, Cinemascope, 35mm, and video. We had probably every format you can imagine in the cutting room, but obviously we could only work on one format so everything was transferred on to $\frac{3}{4}$ inch videotape and we cut on that. However, we had to devise a system to keep track of all the material, because what I cut on videotape ultimately had to end up on 35mm film. My assistant needed to look at the cut videotape and work out where each bit of super 8mm, 16mm, etc. had originally come from, get that transferred on to 35mm and re-conform the cut on 35mm. 1,200 optical effects also had to be generated from the correct material and put on to 35mm. It was a nightmare! As with any movie, we screened **JFK** several times. Each time it had to be conformed on to 35mm film from the cut I had done on videotape. When you work on a digital image it is important to conform it on to film and screen it. Then you can re-familiarise yourself with the real size of the screen, see the colour of the film and notice the details that sometimes get lost on a small monitor.

The cutting style on **JFK** was certainly very dynamic. Indeed the beauty of editing this film was that we could jump around from different locations, we could link witnesses, we could link thoughts or theories – all through visual language. The style was influenced and inspired by Oliver Stone's screenplay, by the visuals that he got and by his knowledge, and we just had a field day with that particular movie. The

style or language that you use in editing is dictated by the material that's shot and by the film-maker and his vision. He shoots it that way. In the editing of course you can manipulate it and cut it. Sometimes things do not work out the way they are planned so you find a different solution. Sometimes you discover things in the editing that you were not aware of, but the actual style is determined by the way that it is shot.

For example, at dailies on a Bertolucci film you can see how beautifully he moves his camera. The lyricism and poetry of his images are very stimulating. You don't want to cut it up. It does not have to be fast, because the beauty is contained within the way he shot it. With Bertolucci I found you could cut between two shots moving in different directions and it would not clash – although you would expect it to. The speed is so consistent and correct that you do not notice the cut, and the shots flow together beautifully. During editing you try to reproduce that beauty and to recreate a feeling of movement throughout – connecting the movements, almost musically.

The style of **Gladiator** is completely different from the old Roman epics. It is not shot in an old epic format – big, spectacular and static – rather the battle scene is shot like **Platoon**, like a Vietnam war movie, with hand-held cameras down in the mud with the actors. The film is shot in a very modern way, aware of certain conventions of viewers nowadays. So the approach in the cutting room is different. We could also incorporate digital technology, which was not possible 30 years ago. The tiger fight is an interesting example of modern digital technology affecting the film and

(1–3) **JFK:** "The cutting style on **JFK** was certainly very dynamic. Indeed the beauty of editing this film was that we could jump around from different locations, we could link witnesses, we could link thoughts or theories – all through visual language. The style was influenced and inspired by Oliver Stone's screenplay, by the visuals that he got and by his knowledge, and we just had a field day with that particular movie."

gl_end_110_18
CU Maximus's hand over wheat #2
CGI: Color Treatment

Notes that Pietro made for himself to grasp the essence of **Gladiator** (3): "Although it's an action film, its soul is about a man who wants to go home. Throughout there is a reference to Maximus (the General) as a man of the land who wants to return to his idyllic, family life. It was shot to start with as a close-up of Russell Crowe standing in the middle of a battlefield. For the end Ridley shot a sequence where the gladiator rejoins his dead family in heaven with images of wheat. There was a 'hand over wheat' shot in this end sequence which I saw as a very powerful poetic image which could resonate throughout the whole film (2). So instead, I started the film with this shot and then cut to a close-up of Maximus. It's in his head – that's what he wants to do. The film is about a man who wants to go home. So in the first two shots I state my thesis of the film completely!"

Transhumance – the movement of (earth) livestock & herds/from to different grazing grounds with the changing of the seasons

from one place to another latin trans and humus = earth ground.

transient – a slave
Passing away with time
transitory / fleeting
Passing thru' one place to another

transgression – The violation of a law, command or duty.

Transience also transiency the state of being transient
(death is freedom)
– Colosseum A passageway –

Transformation – – to come of
Transcend / Transcended
Transcending
Transcends
a) To pass beyond (a human limit)
"an emotion that transcends understanding"
b) To exist above and independent of (material experience or the universe
Transcendent /
to excel –
Kant's theory of knowledge, – designating knowledge that is beyond the limits of experience
4) Mathematics – Designating a number not formed by the fundamental arithmetic operation, each performed only a finite number of times
Transcendental (No
3) Mathematics a) Not capable of being determined by any combination of a finite number of equations with

ant. rational integral coefficients.
b) Not expressible as an integer or quotient of integers. –
Said of numbers especially, nonterminating infinite decimals
Transcendentalism / 1) Philosophy:
a) The belief that knowledge of reality is derived from intuitive sources rather than from objective experience –
b) Any doctrine based on the belief, as the philosophy of Kant.
2.

SPIRIT

MIND → BODY

3

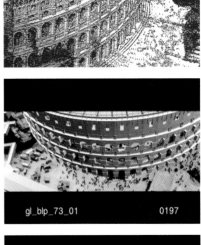

gl_blp_73_01   0197

Pietro sent Ridley a memo which Ridley returned to him with his notes (5) – Scott was shooting in Morocco while Pietro was cutting in London. Wes Sewell, the visual effects editor, was continually developing the computer-generated image shots (based on the original storyboards). The various elements being gradually composited were: the Colosseum; a CGI-created 360-degree turn around the amphitheatre before the Carthage fight; and the tiger fight (6–8). During the cutting process it is good to screen the film with an audience – you sense an audience participate in a film and you can learn a lot. This is an example of a form filled in by a member of the test audience for **Gladiator** (9 overleaf).

6

editing & post-production

7

8

9

the post-production process. The fight involves the gladiator Maximus (played by Russell Crowe) fighting a champion while surrounded by tigers on chains. The fight has been fixed so that the tigers will attack and kill Maximus, so the crew needed to shoot tigers being very aggressive and ferocious right near the two fighters – but the tigers wouldn't do that. They were trained tigers, not ferocious tigers so you had to entice them to jump aggressively. I knew what was needed from the storyboards and I knew I was not getting this from the dailies. I was struggling putting that scene together. I had to go to the visual effects team and tell them that I needed a tiger to jump in a certain way and swipe with its paw. They said we could shoot the tiger behind a blue screen, cut it out and place it between the two fighters. So I went to the set with the stunt co-ordinator and told them exactly what shots of the tiger I needed and from what angle. We had to be careful that these shots of the tiger would match the live action shots that I already had. The special effects (CGI) house then took all the elements, composited the tigers on to the shot with the actors, created the new shots and gave them back to me to cut into the film. As with all composite effects, we fine-tuned for weeks and weeks – the shot going back and forth between the cutting room and the special effects house until we were happy.

However, despite all these changes in film-making style and technology, I think that good storytelling will never change. You can sit by a fire and tell a story which affects your audience. There will always be stories to be told. There will be a different medium, but drama, how you affect emotions and the emotions that come to all of us during life, will always be constant. It will be the same 50 or a 100 years from now. We'll still be jealous, there will still be anger, there will still be love and laughter and we'll still have storytellers. That won't change.

biography

Jill Bilcock was born in Melbourne, Australia. During her summer vacation in 1966, at the age of 18, Jill bought a 16mm Bolex camera and went to China during the cultural revolution to shoot film there. She made a small documentary for CBS from the footage. She then went on to study film at the Swinbourne College of Technology where her final exam film was on Aboriginal human rights issues. Because there was not

jill bilcock

enough time to use the Steenbeck in the college, she cut the film on her kitchen table. The film was subsequently accepted for showing at several film festivals. After college Jill worked in a commercials company and then travelled extensively throughout India and Central and South America. In 1976 she returned to Australia and worked as an assistant on **The Chant of Jimmie Blacksmith** (1978, Fred Schepisi). Her first major feature film as an editor was **A Cry in the Dark** (1988, Fred Schepisi). Since then Jill has cut **Strictly Ballroom** (1992, Baz Luhrmann), **Muriel's Wedding** (1994, P. J. Hogan), **How to Make an American Quilt** (1995, Jocelyn Moorhouse), **William Shakespeare's Romeo & Juliet** (1996, Baz Luhrmann), **Elizabeth** (1998, Shekhar Kapur), **The Dish** (2000, Rob Sitch), **Moulin Rouge** (2001, Baz Luhrmann) and most recently, the as yet untitled Mendes/Zanuck production based on the book, 'The Road to Perdition', starring Tom Hanks, Paul Newman and Jude Law, directed by Sam Mendes.

interview

Someone once asked me how I came to be a film editor, and to be quite honest, I simply put my hand up at art school when the lecturer asked who would be interested in making a film. Maybe editing is not one of the most glamorous of film jobs, but I certainly love it. When I am editing, I listen to what directors say to me even if I disagree. In many ways editing is trying to understand what the director's vision is and then to surprise the director by going further than their vision. For some directors, post-production is a real burden because it takes so long. It is also when they are most vulnerable since they are often physically exhausted at the end of shooting. So it is important that the editor is not like some little dragon snapping and snarling from behind the editing machine! The editor has a key and it opens endless creative doors. It is by opening these doors that you invariably find a new solution to a problem. You always need to be briefed by the director about the essence of a scene – for instance, if they tell you: "I want this character to appear very small and frightened and by the end of this scene to have conquered a fear about her father", then you understand it. Then you can ask yourself, "how am I going to get the best out of this scene?" You will need to know emotionally exactly where you were the previous scene and how that affects the scene you are cutting. You also need to be aware of what will follow the scene you are cutting and how you will maintain the essence of what you are trying to express.

Shekhar Kapur was the director of **Elizabeth** and, being from India, he initially seemed relatively passive compared to other directors who never stop talking and telling you exactly how to do things. Shekhar was very quiet and thoughtful and he just assumed that since I was an editor I would just do what I would do. It was not that Shekhar did not know what he wanted, because he had a very, very strong vision of the movie. I just found it hard to communicate with him at first. After a while I worked out what he was doing – which is crucial in my role as an editor. His most lovable theory was "out of chaos comes order" – so be **Elizabeth**. He always believed in me and working with him was a really great experience. He was quite determined to have me cut **Elizabeth**. During phone conversations before I started on the picture he would say to me, "Jill, you will cut my film. It is destiny."

The first time I worked with Baz Luhrmann was on **Strictly Ballroom**. I met him when he was interviewing for that film. By coincidence I had just been to the opening of *La Bohème*, the opera he had directed. I was very impressed by the opera

and I had an immediate rapport with Baz. It was the beginning of a very special friendship and working relationship. I had not even read the script of **Strictly Ballroom**, but I agreed to cut it simply because I felt that Baz would be able to do it. I had a lot of input into the film and creatively it was very rewarding. When I wanted to push the film further in the cutting room Baz would be there, wanting to go further too. I knew during shooting that it would be something special because of the unselfish attitude and creative energy from all the people involved. **Strictly Ballroom** was cut on film. However, with **Romeo & Juliet** there was absolutely no way that we could have cut it on film, given the detail in it and the very tight schedule within which we were working. Indeed, in many ways the fact that we cut it on a non-linear computer system is what created the style of the movie.

Romeo & Juliet is a film based on language. We were interested in taking William Shakespeare's play and recreating it in a different world, making it for the people that it is about – contemporary 15 and 16 year olds. Hopefully everybody else would come and see it as well. The non-linear system helped me cut sequences together very quickly and rush out on to the set to show Baz – I would be there constantly with tapes in the middle of the shoot. We discussed the film all the time. By cutting material immediately I was able to quickly see what was missing while the crew was still shooting. I would then make up a list of pick-up shots and send them out to the production. On the last three days of shooting, Don McAlpine, the director of photography used to

1

2

(1–2) **Strictly Ballroom** was the first film Jill cut for director Baz Luhrmann: "It is possibly the most complete work that I have done. It is a film that I can still watch and there are not many that I want to watch again."

5

6

7

8

jill bilcock

(1–4) In 1993 Jill cut **Muriel's Wedding** for P. J. Hogan. "It was an exceptional script and a delight to edit. Comedy always seems to work best when it is cut very fast. You can never underestimate how quickly you can cut comedy and get away with it." (5–6) The following year she cut on film **How to Make an American Quilt** for Hogan's wife, Jocelyn Moorhouse. "It looks like it is cut on film, it has a gentle soft look to it." (7–8) Since then Jill has cut films on computer including **Elizabeth** where she brought a dynamic style to costume drama.

editing & post-production

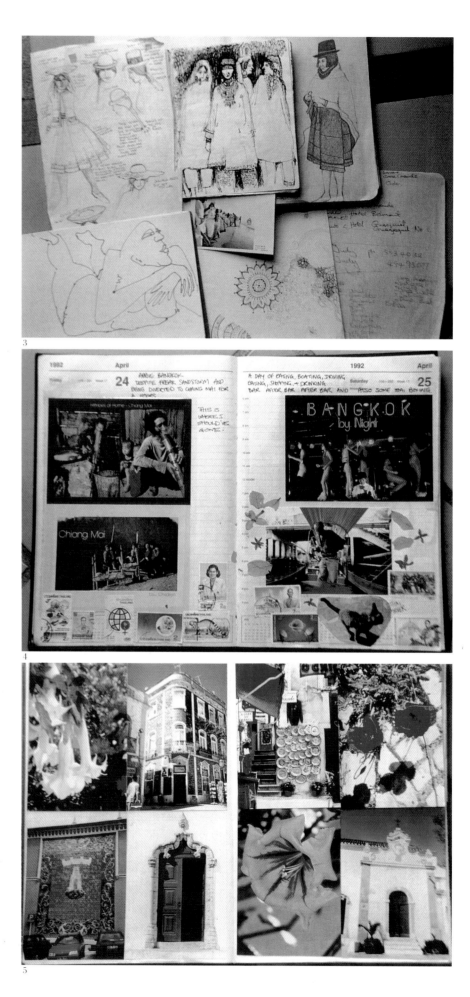

(1–5) Jill enjoys travelling and drawing. "Editing is only an accidental career. I think that if you have an art background, you can pretty well adapt it to anything you like. I would like to do more drawing."

say: "Don't let that woman on the set, she's got another list!" We did a lot of pick-ups due to the fact that I was cutting so quickly and supplying material that we could review. Baz and I have a very similar sense of style and we feel that we know each other very well. We have an exceptionally good creative partnership and a fairly unique working relationship. We share ideas all the time, there is no time given to leisure. While we were in Mexico, at the end of the day I would sometimes go down to the set to discuss the next day's shoot. After viewing rushes together we would often go back to the editing room and look at something I had cut and then discuss the next scene to be done. They were very, very long days.

A lot of the sources of material in **Romeo & Juliet** come from footage other than that shot by the film crew. An example is the riot scene at the beginning of the film. Baz's cook and somebody's girlfriend, and various others had shot some footage on personal video cameras. I went through it all. Then the pieces that I liked were transferred on to film. This material ends up in the movie along with some video footage, and that is why it looks sort of slightly grainy or TV-like. This was deliberate. We wanted to texturally build something distinctive at the beginning of the film, so that when the film starts, you are taken straight away into a very particular kind of world. The music we used, the type of costumes, the setting, the editing – it was all there to take you instantly into this other world. Actually the ratings board helped define the style and the opening of **Romeo & Juliet**. They were not going to give it a PG 13 and one of the reasons was that they found the opening shoot-out too violent. We saw the shoot-out

like an over-the-top spaghetti western where the gang cannot even shoot straight. However, the ratings board did not get the humour. What I did then was speed up more shots and make it even more ridiculous.

Working on computer meant that it was easier to do effect shots or opticals such as speed changes and zoom-ins during the film. The editor cannot try these out in a film cutting room. When you work on film every effect you want must be marked on the film and then sent off to an opticals house. You then wait a day or two for that effect to come back before you see what it looks like. However, on computer you can see almost immediately what a freeze-frame, slow down, speed-up or whatever will look like. Cutting **Romeo & Juliet** on computer certainly produced a lot of effects and you see them scattered throughout the movie. The opening sequence is a zoom-in on a TV set which starts off very small. The TV presenter was shot as one element and then the background of the presenter was added, and then it was all played through a TV. This TV is then re-shot while zooming in. Then that shot becomes a piece of negative for another effect adding another zoom-in on the end in post-production. I wanted it to be an even bigger crash-zoom. I wanted the dots to be enormous, but I was fighting with the opticals department who just did not want to go that far. They kept saying that it would look grainy whereas I kept saying that was the idea. The Jesus images throughout the film are computer generated. They were taken to a tape house in San Francisco and had all kinds of crash-zooms put on and then were scanned back on to film. I used to say to one of my assistants, "find any scraps of film

Fulgencio
CAPULET
Juliet's father

The crash-zooms on the Jesus images were computer generated. The zoom in at the start of the film was a complicated optical effect. The freeze-frames and titles at the start were part of a trashy 1970s' style opening to the movie. This also functioned as a means to introduce the characters otherwise Jill felt the audience would be confused. The fast cutting and speeding up of the film – easy to experiment when cutting on computer – gave a humorous quality to the opening shoot-out, as well as setting the style for the rest of the film. The opening riot scene was shot by Luhrmann's cook among others and contributed to the rough grainy effect: "We wanted to texturally build something into the beginning of the film so that when the film starts you are taken straight into a

editing & post-production

Moulin Rouge (1–5) incorporated many exciting aspects of editing. Jill saw it as "a rich tapestry of colour, shape, exquisite composition, pattern and movement. Sometimes the cutting would be fast to express a particular emotion, but always rhythmically directional so that the sum of the whole should not feel disjointed." Jill spent a lot of time on the shoot working closely with Baz Luhrmann (1, 4–5).

that have strange moves, look for accidents and ends of shots, anything." One person went through the whole film and put together all these scraps. Then we took these "scraps" down to an effects house in San Francisco and made them add as many moves to them as possible. Once the effects house had added their moves we brought them back and we digitised them back on to the Lightworks and added them into the film. I was constantly looking for junk.

We wanted to embrace a lot of styles texturally because the language is so rich and so beautiful. There was a lot of detail in the way the picture looked. In the film if there is a piece of paper that is put on the table it has to have something in the Elizabethan style written on it. This attention to detail had to be maintained all the way through. The cutting had to be the same and that was our means to add texture to the language. The edit was about maintaining visual interest and style and generally taking you on a journey that complements the language, which hopefully we did. One of the assets of the non-linear system was that it created, I think, something that has been described at times as jerky, instant-headache editing. But it was all part of an overall style.

I enjoy cutting low budget films for first time directors. They are of great importance to me because of their passion, commitment, freshness, and their willingness to not be led by the safety of a studio. I like to keep my work unpredictable, varied and culturally diverse – such as Clara Law's **Temptation of a Monk**, which was in Mandarin, and Aboriginal director Richard Frankland's **Harry's War**. First time feature directors I have worked with include Richard Lowenstein on **Dogs in Space**, P. J. Hogan on **Muriel's Wedding**, Baz Luhrmann on **Strictly Ballroom**, Ana Kokkinos on **Head On**, while **The Dish** was Rob Sitch's second low budget independent feature.

Moulin Rouge was a wonderful project as it incorporated so many aspects of editing that excite me – strong, emotional story, comedy, and dance. It is first and foremost a love story, effortlessly told by a fusion of music and dialogue. Our terminology was that we would try to reinvent the musical. I saw it as a rich tapestry of colour, shape, exquisite composition, pattern and movement. Sometimes the cutting would be fast to express a particular emotion, but always rhythmically directional so that the sum of the whole should not feel disjointed. All quick cuts should be part of an overall plan in rhythmic story-telling integrated seamlessly with slower emotionally driven scenes. At all times my editing is driven by story, not by style.

biography

William Chang can remember watching movies as a young boy growing up in Hong Kong: "I was already fascinated by how the story was told in a series of separate pictures put together in a particular way. What I did not know then was that I was watching an editor at work." William went on to study film in Canada and since his return to Hong Kong has not only worked as an editor, but has also been one of the

william chang

most sought-after production designers and art directors in the Hong Kong film industry. His many credits include **Homecoming** (1984) and **Red Dust** (1990) for Yim Ho; **The Peach-Blossom Land** (1992) for Stan Lai; and **Zu: Warriors from the Magic Mountain** (1983) and **The Blade** (1995) for Tsui Hark. He is responsible for the production design on all of Wong Kar-Wai's films and has edited all of them since **Ashes of Time** (1994), including **Fallen Angels** (1995), **Happy Together** (1997) and **In the Mood for Love** (2000).

interview

Both production design and editing are about the "look" of a film. While production design creates the visual look, editing creates the emotional look of the film. I edit the same way I design. I go by my emotion and a sense of rhythm. All the "techniques" I use are based on these two basic principles – emotions and rhythm. The rhythm is not a repetitive metric rhythm as in music or classical poetry. I just feel there is an intrinsic tempo in a movie that glues that movie together. A modern poem does not observe the same rigid rules that used to govern the way in which poems were written. Yet it still has a rhythm, although a more subtle rhythm than older poems. It is this rhythm that makes it a poem.

What excites me with editing is the unpredictability of what will result from the whole process and the capability of "manipulating" (not in the negative sense) human emotions, so to convey the director's intention and ideas for the film. I start by going through all the rushes and selecting moments

William uses techniques such as freeze-frames in his editing. For example, in **Happy Together** during the farewell scene between Fai and his co-worker in the restaurant there are two freezes of the handshake (4–5), as well as slow motion used in some shots (7–8). William created the impression that the embrace of the two after the handshake was also a freeze-frame although it was not. "The two freeze-frames plus the illusory freeze artificially prolong a feeling; they create a false sense that the moment is lasting, maybe even permanent. But the reality was these two men were perhaps never to see each other again marking the finality of the relationship. The freeze-frames serve as a 'set-up' for the finality to convey the thought that in life relationships, emotions and sentimentality are really quite fleeting and ephemeral."

that move me – which could be a frame, a piece of dialogue, or just an image. Then I'll make different collages with this material. The moment when I have the feeling that I've got something "right", i.e. something expresses the essence of the film, then I'll take that as my "editing point". I will then rearrange all the material centring on that point. If, unfortunately, the material that I've chosen is not enough for a complete film, I'll go back to the rushes that I put aside at the very beginning and add them to the edit as necessary. Editing is pretty much like cooking – you are limited according to the ingredients you have. Sometimes spices are needed for the process!

I do not cut a film in a sequential order following the story-line. On any particular day I would be drawn to certain scenes. I cut the scenes I am editing as if they were self-contained. I may try several versions of a scene, but I always end up with the version that affects me emotionally the most in the first instance. It is like how the first impression of a person is the one that affects you the most. For me, the editing process is about constant changes and constant demands on your inner creativity. I will look at the scenes I have edited over and over again, until I get the feeling that I am watching a film and not just a collection of what I refer to as "editing points". Since my approach to editing is instinctive and emotional, it is not difficult for me to decide what should be left on the cutting room floor. I seldom agonise over picking which version to use. The tough decision comes only after I have all the scenes cut and I am ready to make them into a whole. Since Wong Kar-Wai's films are not in the traditional

narrative form where one proceeds from A to Z in a linear, story-telling fashion, there can be any number of ways to tell his stories. This means that we often spend more time discussing whether the last scene should be the opening one or whether the middle scene should really be the last, rather than deciding how a particular scene should be edited or re-edited.

Some may believe the roles of being simultaneously the art director and editor could clash. But they never do. I do these two jobs as if I am two different people. When I design, I don't think about editing at all. I think if there is any conflict at all, it gets resolved before filming begins. Wong Kar-Wai and I talk so much about his script and his idea that by the time shooting begins, I invariably feel I know quite well what he and I both wish to convey in his movie. I don't use "techniques" consciously as a tool. My idols have shown me in their work that there can be no rules if you know what you want to say in a film. Any "technique" is okay if it gets you closer to what you feel the scene is about. I try not to allow conventional views of how a scene should be cut together to influence me on how I present a scene or sequence of scenes.

Let me talk about jump-cuts which many have asked me about their significance, as if I was trying to create a "style", send a "message" or make a "statement". The simple answer is none of the above. Every cut is a jump-cut to me. To put it another way, a jump-cut is just another cut. I do not consciously differentiate between a cut and a jump-cut. A cut, any cut, is to collapse, to condense the time between two

William Chang frequently uses "jump-cuts" in his editing rather than worrying about making smooth invisible edits that maintain the flow of continuity. In **Happy Together** (1–5) the use of jump-cuts can be seen in the montage of café fronts (3) and the scene where Ho is dancing (2, 5).

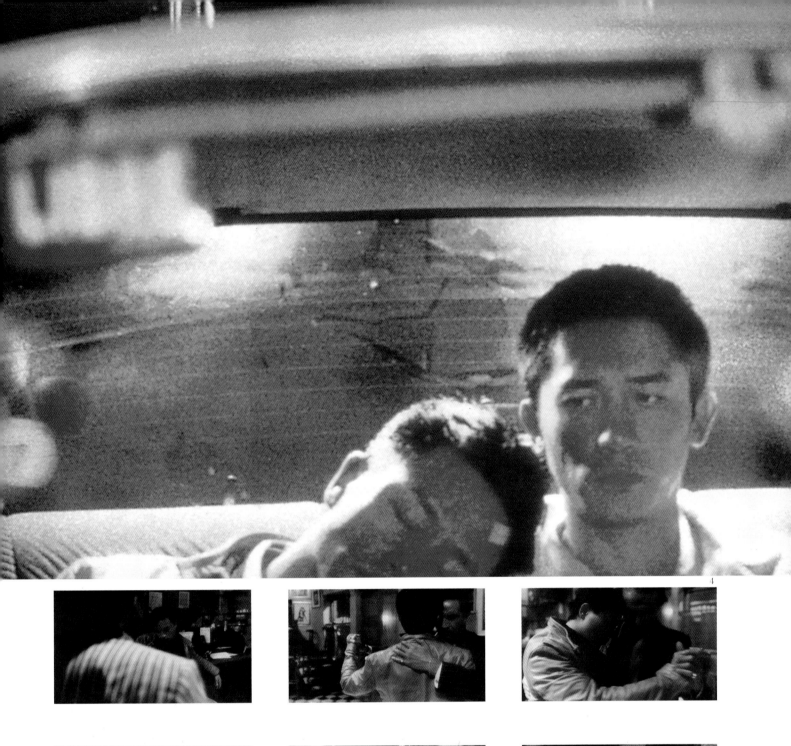

4

5

The scene where Lai commits murder in **Fallen Angels** is also edited with jump-cuts. These two sequences show the frames at either side of the cut, allowing you to see where the "jump" occurs.

2

3

events. A movie, by its nature, has to economise the usage of time to tell a story. I view a jump-cut just like any other cut – its function is to economise.

To me, much of what is shown on the screen seems redundant to the story. In the films I edit, I want to get the irrelevant information out of the way. It clutters and muddles up the strength of a scene. I want to get to the point quickly. Therefore I would not hesitate to use "jumps" in a conversation if I feel the spoken words are irrelevant to the emotions of the scene. And I would not use a cut-away as a bridge between one shot and another as it is usually done in "conventional" films. Anything that is irrelevant to the moment I disallow in my editing.

There is also a philosophical angle to using jump-cuts: I believe so much that life is essentially ephemeral. You touch it and it is gone. You cannot hold on to it. Moments in life are like that. They are here and then they are gone. Life is just a sequence of such moments. Memory is also essentially ephemeral and so are relationships. Even in a long relationship how you felt towards each other in the beginning is usually not how you feel today or tomorrow. This is true both in a long-term or a short-term relationship. In fact the length of a relationship is completely unrelated to the strength of feelings. The intensity of a short relationship can often be stronger than that of a long liaison. Jump-cuts are a reminder and a manifestation of this basic fact of life. It is in this context that one should look at all my "techniques", be they jump-cuts, freeze-frames, opticals, slow motions, or inter-

cutting between black and colour. They are not "styles" I deliberately use to distinguish our films from others. They are used to bring out the emotional essence of a particular situation. Indeed I cannot emphasise enough that finding the emotional essence of the story is the foundation of my work.

163

william chang

biography

Skip Lievsay was born in North Carolina, but moved to New York at the age of 11. He started working in the construction industry in the 1960s and hoped to go on to study architecture. However, during a recession in construction during the early 1970s he met up with an independent film-maker who offered him work on a low-budget feature. In the true spirit of low-budget film-making he did everything from

skip lievsay

making the coffee to marking up the clapperboard and helping the editor. More work in film followed including a stint with a post-production firm, which made up TV versions of films. Skip gravitated towards sound editing which was where the work was at the time. In 1989 he got together with other sound editors and they set up C5 – a sound post-production facility in Manhattan. His credits include films for the Coen Brothers (**Blood Simple** (1983), **Barton Fink** (1991), and **The Barber** (working title) (2001)); Martin Scorsese (**After Hours** (1985), **The Color of Money** (1986), **The Last Temptation of Christ** (1988), and **Cape Fear** (1991)); Barry Sonnenfeld (**Men in Black** (1997) and **Wild Wild West** (1999)); Jonathan Demme (**The Silence of the lambs** (1990)); and Spike Lee (**Do the Right Thing** (1989), **Mo' Better Blues** (1990), and **Malcolm X** (1992)).

interview

Basically the job of the sound editor is to take all of the material that comprises a soundtrack (except for the music), organise it, edit it and prepare it for the dub where it will all be mixed together. It would be natural to think that all these sounds should have been picked up by the sound recordist during the shoot, however, microphones tend to be directional and they block out all ambient sounds. This is exactly what you want because the aim of the recordist is to get the actor's performance at all costs. The emphasis during the production is on the actors and not on the sound effects. It is much easier to add a footstep sound six weeks later than to add an actor. That is the most efficient way of doing it and that is where the sound editors come in. Thus the original sound as was recorded by the sound recordist when they shot the film is only the starting point for us. This sound makes up the dialogue tracks. However, these dialogue tracks are augmented with many other tracks containing foley, sound effects, ADR, atmosphere tracks and special sound design recordings. Meanwhile the music department is working independently with the composer, recording music and gathering the existing songs that will be used. Each of these different kinds of sounds has its own specialist editor. Then there are assistants who help all these editors do their job. There is a lot of work to do. On big movies like **Men in Black** and **Wild Wild West** the sound department was working for six months. Smaller movies can be got in and out of here in a month.

The dialogue editor is responsible for a lot of technical work ensuring that the dialogue tracks are smooth and do not jar. Another big responsibility of the dialogue editor is to figure out what lines are no good. Dialogue is no good, for example, if you hear a big bang in the middle of a character's line. Now if the bang is a door closing and you can see the actor close the door that is fine, but in many cases it is an unwanted background noise. Even if the sound is part of the story it can still be too loud and blocking out the words. In such cases you need to re-record the line without the noise. The actors are brought back to do this and the process is called ADR or looping. Actually in some of the big modern movies that you see in the cinema 80–90 per cent of the dialogue you hear will be ADR. I think the average would be around 30 per cent, which means that when you see a movie about a third of the dialogue was re-recorded and replaced.

A lot of the locations that Spike Lee and Martin Scorsese shoot are noisy, therefore a lot of the track has to be replaced. There is a lot of ADR in a Spike Lee film, usually over 50 per cent, though sometimes it can be as much as 75 per cent. Scorsese's **GoodFellas** (1990) was a good example of a film needing ADR because it was shot on location in New York. Also De Niro is a very internal actor so he does not project which makes it even harder again for the sound recordist. Despite these problems Scorsese does not like to do looping. It is very difficult to get as much emotion on an ADR stage six months later as you did during the original well-rehearsed performance. Most actors do not know how to loop well enough to repeat the same emotion as on set. Even during the shoot the director may accept that dialogue will need to be re-recorded. An example is when special effects are creating noise on set. At the end of **Cape Fear** De Niro is drowning in this huge storm. The storm was created by wind machines. These are like huge noisy aircraft propellers so it was always clear that we would have to loop. As De Niro is drowning he is "speaking in tongues" or babbling. When he came back to re-record the dialogue he took bottles of water and was gurgling and spitting out the water as he said the lines. This was to make it sound like a man drowning! During the ADR recording for **The Color of Money** Paul Newman did not want to do some lines. I said: "it's a very important line but none of us can understand what you're saying so we need to re-record it." Newman gave me a look and said: "OK, I'll do it if we can do it outside." So we went to the roof of the building and I took a mike with me. This line was partially off-camera, so the lip sync was easy to cheat. The sound was a great match because we recorded it outside like the production dialogue.

1

			CAPE FEAR	Online #	
Cape Fear Scratch Fx 1	D01	01.	punch assortment: 12 hits, face and body		Cape Fear
Cape Fear Scratch Fx 1	D01	02.	kick assortment: 4 kicks		Cape Fear
Cape Fear Scratch Fx 1	D01	03.	fighting, with punches		Cape Fear
Cape Fear Scratch Fx 1	D01	04.	body falls: on leaves, carpet, bed, car, floor, dirt, gravel,		Cape Fear
Cape Fear Scratch Fx 1	D01	05.	swamp: frogs		Cape Fear
Cape Fear Scratch Fx 1	D01	06.	swamp: spooky insects and birds, jungle		Cape Fear
Cape Fear Scratch Fx 1	D01	07	swamp: insects		Cape Fear
Cape Fear Scratch Fx 1	D01	08	swamp: insects		Cape Fear
Cape Fear Scratch Fx 1	D01	09	swamp: insects, wider		Cape Fear
Cape Fear Scratch Fx 1	D01	10.	gunshots: interior pistol shots (sb 1-3-1,2,3,4)		Cape Fear
Cape Fear Scratch Fx 1	D01	11.	gunshots: exterior pistol shots (sb 1-21-2,3,4,)		Cape Fear
Cape Fear Scratch Fx 1	D01	12.	racquetball game, shots and fs, mvmt		Cape Fear
Cape Fear Scratch Fx 1	D01	13.	racquetball serves		Cape Fear
Cape Fear Scratch Fx 1	D01	14.	light switches, 3x		Cape Fear
Cape Fear Scratch Fx 1	D01	15.	digital watch beeps		Cape Fear
Cape Fear Scratch Fx 1	D01	16.	s185-1 seq. beep @ 9' (rain)		Cape Fear
Cape Fear Scratch Fx 1	D01	17.	s185-2 seq. beep @ 9' (wind)		Cape Fear
Cape Fear Scratch Fx 1	D01	18.	s185-3 seq. beep @ 9' (crash)		Cape Fear
Cape Fear Scratch Fx 1	D01	19.	s185-4 seq. beep @ 9' (thunder)		Cape Fear
Cape Fear Scratch Fx 1	D01	20.	s185-5 seq. beep @ 100 (gunshots)		Cape Fear
Cape Fear Scratch Fx 1	D01	21.	s185-5 seq. beep @ 220 (crash)		Cape Fear
Cape Fear Scratch Fx 1	D01	22	s185-5 seq. beep @ 320 (crash)		Cape Fear
Cape Fear Scratch Fx 1	D01	23.	s185-5 seq. beep @ 150 (storm)		Cape Fear
Cape Fear Scratch Fx 1	D01	24.	s187-1 seq. beep @ 545 (rain + thunder)		Cape Fear
Cape Fear Scratch Fx 1	D01	25.	s11-1 seq. beep @ 590 (racquetball)		Cape Fear
Cape Fear Scratch Fx 1	D01	26.	s11-1 seq. beep @ 85 (prison fx)		Cape Fear
Cape Fear Scratch Fx 1	D01	27.	s11-1 seq. beep @ 180 (thunder)		Cape Fear
Cape Fear Scratch Fx 1	D01	28.	police station atmos		Cape Fear

3

			CAPE FEAR	Online #	
Cape Fear Boat & Rain Fx	D05	01.	drag boat on dirt and rock, scraping and banging (3:00)		Cape Fear
Cape Fear Boat & Rain Fx	D05	08.	drag boat on rock with water (1:00)		Cape Fear
Cape Fear Boat & Rain Fx	D05	09.	drag on gravel, long scrapes (:45)		Cape Fear
Cape Fear Boat & Rain Fx	D05	10.	drag and bang on rocks, bird in bg, much bigger bangs		Cape Fear
Cape Fear Boat & Rain Fx	D05	11.	drag boat on gravel, wood (:20)		Cape Fear
Cape Fear Boat & Rain Fx	D05	12.	drop boat onto dock, then onto water (1:00)		Cape Fear
Cape Fear Boat & Rain Fx	D05	15.	scrape boat on a log in the water, watch the bird (2:30)		Cape Fear
Cape Fear Boat & Rain Fx	D05	17.	crash into sticks on the shore (3:00)		Cape Fear
Cape Fear Boat & Rain Fx	D05	21.	toss boat onto water, drop boat onto water, rocks, sticks		Cape Fear
Cape Fear Boat & Rain Fx	D05	34.	boat banging on rocks, wood; slide, banging (:30)		Cape Fear
Cape Fear Boat & Rain Fx	D05	35.	drag wooden boat on gravel, long hunks (1:30)		Cape Fear
Cape Fear Boat & Rain Fx	D05	39.	toss wooden boat onto rocks (:30)		Cape Fear
Cape Fear Boat & Rain Fx	D05	41.	wooden boat scrape, bang on rocks (:30)		Cape Fear
Cape Fear Boat & Rain Fx	D05	42.	toss boat onto rocks, water (:15)		Cape Fear
Cape Fear Boat & Rain Fx	D05	43.	boats at dock, sloshing-lapping water (1:40)		Cape Fear
Cape Fear Boat & Rain Fx	D05	44.	toss wooden boat onto rocks (:30)		Cape Fear
Cape Fear Boat & Rain Fx	D05	49.	dragging boat around on rocks, wrenching break, toss		Cape Fear
Cape Fear Boat & Rain Fx	D05	67.	board breaks (:20)		Cape Fear
Cape Fear Boat & Rain Fx	D05	69.	toss boat onto rocks (:30)		Cape Fear
Cape Fear Boat & Rain Fx	D05	73.	boat launching, splash-thunk (1:00)		Cape Fear
Cape Fear Boat & Rain Fx	D05	79.	underwater crunching, rocks, gurgling, klunks, some om		Cape Fear
Cape Fear Boat & Rain Fx	D05	81.	6hp motorboat start, idle, away – underwater (1:00)		Cape Fear
Cape Fear Boat & Rain Fx	D05	82.	underwater boat hitting rocks, splashes (:45)		Cape Fear
Cape Fear Boat & Rain Fx	D05	82.	underwater anchor drop, drag (:30)		Cape Fear
Cape Fear Boat & Rain Fx	D05	82.	underwater rock scraping, splashing water (2:00)		Cape Fear
Cape Fear Boat & Rain Fx	D05	82.	rain on the roof, interior, variety of textures (1:30)		Cape Fear
Cape Fear Boat & Rain Fx	D05	82.	rain on the roof, as above, then heavier drops (1:50)		Cape Fear
Cape Fear Boat & Rain Fx	D05	82.	rain on window glass, interior, steady, wooshes (1:25)		Cape Fear

4

In **Sleepy Hollow** there were thousands of thunderclaps (1–2). This was very much part of the design of the movie since it was very Gothic, like an old-fashioned horror film. "After a while you get bored to tears hearing the same stuff over and over again so you have to have hundreds of different thunderclaps so that you can vary it." Skip would have access to many kinds of thunderclaps in his library (3–4). For **Cape Fear** (5–6) Skip actually went out to New Mexico for a weekend to record more thunder.

2

5

6

1

2

In **Men in Black** (1–3) a space ship crashes in front of the two heroes and continues to roll forwards towards them, like it is going to squash them, before it comes to a halt. The sound had to seem authentic so that the audience would feel the ship could crush the two heroes. The effect ended up being a combination of many sounds e.g. an earthquake rumbling, thunder, metal dragging, rock, scraping and screeching. All these sounds were layered together, mixed, manipulated and pitched down with all sorts of processing to create the effect. "A sound like that does not exist, so there are no recordings. So you create a sound effect which you know helps the story."

3

A lot of actors possibly do not realise the need for ADR. Most of the actors who are good at it understand what is going on and they know how important it is for them to do well. There is nothing worse than a dramatic scene, which has to be re-recorded for technical reasons, but the actors cannot get back their performance – and so the scene falls down. This is a real dilemma. If you stick with the original you say: "The emotion is great and everyone is hitting their lines, but this background noise is unbearable and takes you right out of the scene." Then when you use looped dialogue instead of the noisy original you go: "Oh man, this performance sucks, these actors are terrible." So it is hard to decide which to choose. Some actors like Al Pacino do a really good loop. Pacino is aware of how powerful a tool looping is because he has done it for so many years and he has the skill to be able to memorise his performance. He is also the only actor that I have worked with who starts off with one performance and might end up with something else. He can really change his performance with looping to benefit the film.

The editing of effects can be divided into three distinct categories. Firstly you have the background ambient sounds. These are natural sounds such as wind, storm sounds, crickets and so on. Secondly there are hard effects like the sound of a door closing, a car passing by, explosions or a kettle. Finally you have foley. This is all the little sounds characters make like footsteps, moving a dinner fork across a plate and putting it down, taking a coat off and sitting down. Each of these different kinds of effects is done for various reasons. The atmospheres are usually done to make the film considerably more realistic. The hard effects are usually done to make the film more dramatic. And the foley is usually done to fill in the sounds that are not recorded in production. The foley is recorded by playing the film to the foley artists who are recorded as they match the movements on the screen like footsteps, a jacket coming off, a fork on a plate and so on. The skill is to pick the right sound for even what may seem like a simple effect. For example, every door on the planet has probably a different sound, each one so subtly different. Certainly there are hundreds of different types of doors: metal doors, glass doors, church doors, refrigerator doors and so on. As well, there are many perspectives on each door from close-up to far away. This means there are millions of permutations of just a door opening and closing.

An effect must support what is happening with the image, because sound adds to the overall impact in such a profound way. Since **Men in Black** deals with aliens there were a lot of sounds that do not exist. We had to work to create something new. For the weapons we made sounds using a combination of mechanical noises, saw sounds, cannons and gun shots. There was a big alien in the film like a huge insect. I gave it a voice through a combination of various sounds, mostly bear and horse sounds which I processed by slowing them down, changing the pitch and adding a bass element. The insect also had unique footsteps and a cracking sound whenever it turned its head. I tried to make it feel like how such a creature would sound if it were walking around. It was an interesting challenge because you are trying to create a reality from something that does not exist.

editing & post-production

Online Edit | Find All | Find Take | All Online Fx | Rel Data | Oops Note | Print All

SILENCE OF THE LAMBS				Online #	
Whale Fx	C73	01	whale fx slowed down deep heavy underwater activity		Silence Of The Lambs
Whale Fx	C73	02	whale fx reverberant deep heavy groans moans		Silence Of The Lambs
Whale Fx	C73	03	whale fx real thing squeals pings yells barks snorts		Silence Of The Lambs
Whale Fx	C73	04	whale fx uderwater ships hull sci fi		Silence Of The Lambs
Animal Fx 01	C74	1	hawk shock scream		Silence Of The Lambs
Animal Fx 01	C74	2	lower voice 3rd take very low reverse rooster		Silence Of The Lambs
Animal Fx 01	C74	3	low rolling drone long take cougar purr		Silence Of The Lambs
Animal Fx 01	C74	4	long low drone cougar purr		Silence Of The Lambs
Animal Fx 01	C74	5	low build with some upper stuff elk		Silence Of The Lambs
Animal Fx 01	C74	6	single low roar with high buzzing moose		Silence Of The Lambs
Animal Fx 01	C74	7	swish blast with low bug accent rattle snake		Silence Of The Lambs
Animal Fx 01	C74	8	3 blasts bug accent rattler		Silence Of The Lambs
Animal Fx 01	C74	9	long rolling drone wolf		Silence Of The Lambs
Sotl Pfx Dat 01	C75	01	gunnery range din/quantico training center/multiple	SIL001	Silence Of The Lambs
Sotl Pfx Dat 01	C75	02	gunnery range interior din/multiple firearms firing from	SIL002	Silence Of The Lambs
Sotl Pfx Dat 01	C75	03	gunnery range /medium distance firing range shots	SIL003	Silence Of The Lambs
Sotl Pfx Dat 01	C75	04	firing range/100's of rounds fired at once / sounds like	SIL004	Silence Of The Lambs
Sotl Pfx Dat 01	C75	05	gunfire singles with woodsy ring out metallic shell clinks		Silence Of The Lambs
Sotl Pfx Dat 01	C75	06	gunfire single shots mic too close for digital no balls		Silence Of The Lambs
Sotl Pfx Dat 01	C75	07	gunfire single shots too close for digital some		Silence Of The Lambs
Sotl Pfx Dat 01	C75	08	gunfire single shots too close for digital some		Silence Of The Lambs
Sotl Pfx Dat 01	C75	09	gunnery range atmos instructor on pa big burst of		Silence Of The Lambs
Sotl Pfx Dat 01	C75	10	gunnery range atmos instructor on pa big burst of		Silence Of The Lambs
Sotl Pfx Dat 01	C75	11	gunnery range interior distant shots sound good close	SIL005	Silence Of The Lambs
Sotl Pfx Dat 01	C75	12	walla/building lobby/mixed group/50 people	SIL006	Silence Of The Lambs
Sotl Pfx Dat 01	C75	13	gym atmos– voices clapping mvmt (relay race)		Silence Of The Lambs
Sotl Pfx Dat 01	C75	14	gym atmos– combat class intructor and class voices om		Silence Of The Lambs
Sotl Pfx Dat 01	C75	15	exercise room training machines weight klunks		Silence Of The Lambs

1

2

3

For the murderer's lair in **The Silence of the Lambs** (1–3) Skip and Eugene Gearty wanted to create a unique and menacing atmosphere. They did this by processing many sounds including jungle sounds, rain plops and guitar feedback which can be seen on the track list (1).

5

Crowd sounds will also be re-recorded in post-production and built up by the sound editor. In the scenes in **Malcolm X** where Malcolm makes speeches (4–5), Skip recreated the cheering by bringing in a hundred extras and recording them responding to the speeches as they were played to them. These cheers were then cut into the soundtrack to match the picture.

4

Eugene Gearty, Skip's colleague at C5, had to come up with new sounds for the punches during the fight sequences in **Crouching Tiger, Hidden Dragon** (1–4). "The idea was to make the fight sequences sound as 'un-Hollywood' as possible so we recorded new whooshes, impacts and cloth rustles." The other challenge was to create a specific sound for the "Green Destiny" sword (1, 3–4). "Ang Lee wanted a breathy slicing sound that would give the sense of a paper-thin wispy blade able to slice through metal." This sound was developed using a glass harmonica and a water phone. When the original dialogue recorded on location is too noisy it will have to be replaced. On a film like **GoodFellas** (5–13), shot on location, a lot of dialogue may

3

4

8

9

10

14

15

16

need to be replaced. The actors are then brought into the studio to record this. The sound editors will lay in selected takes from the looping session in sync with the picture. "There is a very good example of how ADR works in **Singin' in the Rain** (14–16). The actress in the film is a great dancer and looks good, but her voice is terrible. Therefore they hire another actress to replace her voice. The actor is brought back to a recording studio where they repeat the lines to relevant clips of film made up from the original material by the ADR editor. Through professional skill and repetition, they get the performance to sound like the original and also make it lip sync with the film."

Title: **The Barber - BGs/FX DIAL/PFX** - Version: **Reel 7**
Editor: **Eugene Gearty**

p.1 (p.1a of 2a (1))

BG-1/2	BG-3/4	FX-1/2	FX-3/4
8+15 NARR9-01-GAIN	8+15 NARR9-01-GAIN	8+15 NARR9-01-GAIN	8+15 NARR9-01-GAIN
12+00 UNDERWATER ATMOS(R) → 44+03	12+00 BG-B(L)-01 → 44+03		
124+12 PRISON ATMOS W/VOX(L) → 147+07		124+10 GAVEL SLAM(L) → 133+07	
621+02 FX-A(L)-01		483+12 LIGHTS-OUT KA-CHUNKER(L) → 492+04	478+00 LIGHT BELL RING(L) → 490+00
→ 569+08	569+07 crickets/gnff pack--CD1054/29.L	569+05 Johnny Front Door O/C--RBY265 → 376+08	
		592+07 SPACESHIPPER ARRIVER(L) → 639+00	591+13 THERMIN RIPOFF(L) → 645+08
643+05 FX-A(L)-01	→ 645+03	640+14 Johnny Front Door O/C--RBY265 → 643+05	
683+00			

WildSync System L.L.C. -- http://www.wildsync.com

1

Title: **The Barber - BGs/FX DIAL/PFX** - Version: **Reel 7**
Editor: **Eugene Gearty**

p.2 (p.2a of 2a (2))

BG-1/2	BG-3/4	FX-1/2	FX-3/4
643+05 FX-A(L)-01	673+02 CHAIR ROOM BUZZ (L)		674+15 Cairo Jail Door O/C 3X--RBY382.L → 677+01
→ 683+00		675+05 DOOR-SQUEAKER(L) → 681+07	
		690+04 DOOR-SQUEAK(L) → 701+03	693+15 Cairo Jail Door O/C 3X--RBY382.L → 701+12
839+06 NARR9-01-GAIN	→ 839+06	818+02 SPACESHIP ARRIVE(L) → 839+06	818+03 THERMIN RIPOFF(L) → 839+06

WildSync System L.L.C. -- http://www.wildsync.com

2

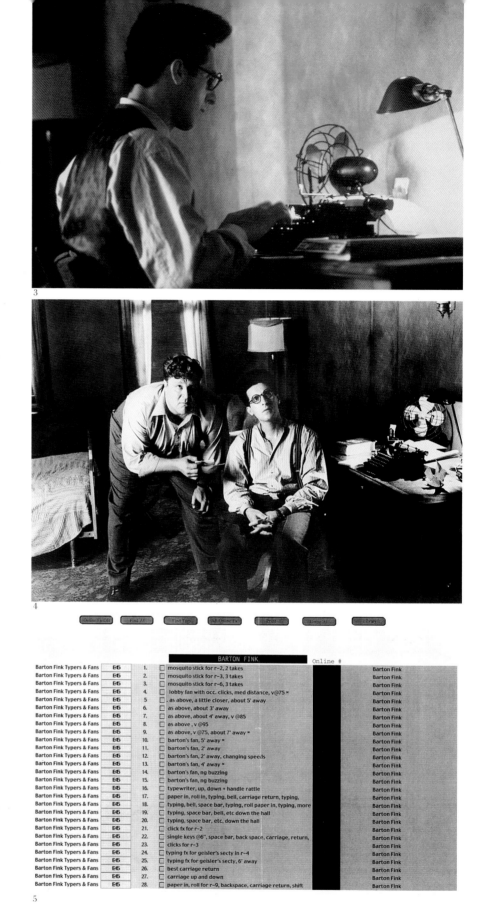

3

4

Online Fx DB · Find All · Find Tags · All Online Fx · Print · Untag All · Library

BARTON FINK   Online #

Barton Fink Typers & Fans	BF6	1.	☐ mosquito stick for r-2, 2 takes	Barton Fink
Barton Fink Typers & Fans	BF6	2.	☐ mosquito stick for r-3, 3 takes	Barton Fink
Barton Fink Typers & Fans	BF6	3.	☐ mosquito stick for r-6, 3 takes	Barton Fink
Barton Fink Typers & Fans	BF6	4.	☐ lobby fan with occ. clicks, med distance, v@75 *	Barton Fink
Barton Fink Typers & Fans	BF6	5.	☐ as above, a little closer, about 5' away	Barton Fink
Barton Fink Typers & Fans	BF6	6.	☐ as above, about 3' away	Barton Fink
Barton Fink Typers & Fans	BF6	7.	☐ as above, about 4' away, v @85	Barton Fink
Barton Fink Typers & Fans	BF6	8.	☐ as above, v @95	Barton Fink
Barton Fink Typers & Fans	BF6	9.	☐ as above, v @75, about 7' away *	Barton Fink
Barton Fink Typers & Fans	BF6	10.	☐ barton's fan, 5' away *	Barton Fink
Barton Fink Typers & Fans	BF6	11.	☐ barton's fan, 2' away	Barton Fink
Barton Fink Typers & Fans	BF6	12.	☐ barton's fan, 2' away, changing speeds	Barton Fink
Barton Fink Typers & Fans	BF6	13.	☐ barton's fan, 4' away *	Barton Fink
Barton Fink Typers & Fans	BF6	14.	☐ barton's fan, ng buzzing	Barton Fink
Barton Fink Typers & Fans	BF6	15.	☐ barton's fan, ng buzzing	Barton Fink
Barton Fink Typers & Fans	BF6	16.	☐ typewriter, up, down + handle rattle	Barton Fink
Barton Fink Typers & Fans	BF6	17.	☐ paper in, roll in, typing, bell, carriage return, typing,	Barton Fink
Barton Fink Typers & Fans	BF6	18.	☐ typing, bell, space bar, typing, roll paper in, typing, more	Barton Fink
Barton Fink Typers & Fans	BF6	19.	☐ typing, space bar, bell, etc down the hall	Barton Fink
Barton Fink Typers & Fans	BF6	20.	☐ typing, space bar, etc, down the hall	Barton Fink
Barton Fink Typers & Fans	BF6	21.	☐ click fx for r-2	Barton Fink
Barton Fink Typers & Fans	BF6	22.	☐ single keys @6", space bar, back space, carriage, return,	Barton Fink
Barton Fink Typers & Fans	BF6	23.	☐ clicks for r-3	Barton Fink
Barton Fink Typers & Fans	BF6	24.	☐ typing fx in geisler's secty in r-4	Barton Fink
Barton Fink Typers & Fans	BF6	25.	☐ typing fx for geisler's secty, 6' away	Barton Fink
Barton Fink Typers & Fans	BF6	26.	☐ best carriage return	Barton Fink
Barton Fink Typers & Fans	BF6	27.	☐ carriage up and down	Barton Fink
Barton Fink Typers & Fans	BF6	28.	☐ paper in, roll for r-9, backspace, carriage return, shift	Barton Fink

5

The track list for **Barton Fink** (3–5) shows some of the typing and fan sound effects used in the film. These dubbing charts (1–2) show some of the sound effects laid at the end (or the final "reel") of the Coen Brothers' film **The Barber** (working title). The numbers refer to feet, so at 675 feet into the reel there is a Theremin sound, a chair room buzz, a door squeak and a separate jail door. These four tracks are only a fraction of those available. Chief sound editor was Eugene Gearty and Skip mixed the tracks.

You can also change reality with sound. In **Barton Fink** we decided John Goodman's hotel room should be like a big and isolated vacuum. I made this sound so that whenever he opened the door you could hear the air rushing in. It sounded like the air was being sucked from the hallway and through his door into the room. I recorded this effect on the foley stage, which is essentially an airtight room, by jimmying open the door and recording the air rushing through. It was a very literal recording. The Coen brothers had not asked for that sound, it was meant as a joke on my part and I just put it in a few places. Then as the movie progressed Ethan wanted it put in every time the door was opened and closed, which was hundreds of times!

On **The Silence of the Lambs**, Eugene Gearty and I worked together to create not just an effect, but a background. Our main goal was to try and create an atmosphere for the murderer's house and thereby his character. There are many scenes in the film where you see the sort of dungeon that the guy lives in including the climactic scene at the end of the film where he is wearing the night vision goggles and you see the green image of him stalking Jodie Foster. The understanding was that those scenes would be atmospheric, but not necessarily through music. I had a recording of a jungle atmosphere, with all different types of animals, crickets and birds. We also had these plopping rain sounds and other sounds created with guitar feedback. The sounds were processed by slowing them down, adding reverb and using filters. By layering these sounds we created this surrealistic atmosphere with an unknown organic sound. The essential goal was to create a different kind of reality for this guy's lair. We felt if we could pull that off it would hype the drama and the suspense. Some of the effects we use I will get from our library of sounds. We have built this up over the years by keeping effects from all the films we have worked on. There are also commercial libraries of sound effects made up by other companies. These are usually fairly specialised and you are lucky if you can match them back to a movie, but they are good to have as a reference. However, rather than just using existing recordings edited together it is visually more efficient and you get a better sound for the movie if you try to imitate that actual event. In **Mo' Better Blues** there were a lot of performances in nightclubs, so we decided to recreate a nightclub atmosphere in a recording studio. We brought hundreds of extras into a big recording studio, sat them down at tables and recorded them with over 25 microphones. This meant that the nightclub atmosphere was very realistic and just right for those scenes.

As the sound supervisor you are answerable to the picture and to the wishes of the director. We try to prepare sounds that we think work. The sounds must also help the director create his or her vision. Then we bring all the different elements of sound that we have laid to the stage mix. Once you get to that point you know it is totally out of your control – unless you happen to be the mixer. Once our soundtracks reach the mixing desk console it is up to the mixer and the director. Together they will come up with the final sound that the audience will hear.

biography

The young Mark Berger developed an imagination based on sound while listening to radio dramas like the *Lone Ranger*. He spent nights hidden underneath the bedclothes so that his parents would not see the red pilot light of the wireless. Later after working on an educational TV project in Colombia he dropped out of graduate school where he had been studying psychology and then brain surgery. He started helping at a

mark berger

local radio station. There he met someone who needed a soundman to shoot a documentary on the Civil Rights movement in Mississippi. After ten months in Mississippi he was put in jail before being run out of town for "rabble rousing"! But Mark had caught the film-making bug and began to work in documentary sound. For a helicopter film of California he needed to show what was happening on the land below through sound alone since the director did not want any narration. Mark was playing this film in Francis Ford Coppola's American Zoetrope in San Francisco when he noticed a man standing at the back listening. The man was Walter Murch and he asked Mark to work with him. Mark went on to mix for Coppola on **The Godfather Part II** (1974). Through a distinguished career Mark has picked up four Oscars for **Apocalypse Now** (1979, Francis Ford Coppola), **The Right Stuff** (1983, Philip Kaufman), **Amadeus** (1984, Milos Forman), and **The English Patient** (1996, Anthony Minghella).

interview

On a basic level the mixer takes all the sound tracks that the editors have prepared and "mixes" them together, deciding how loud each track should be relative to the others. In doing this the mixer is responsible for shaping the entire sound of the film. The same way the art director and the cameraman and the director shape the visual image, the supervising sound editor and the mixer shape the sonic space of the film. The editors are the people who prepare the sounds. The job of the mixer is to put it all together – just like the head chef in a restaurant. In a restaurant you have the salad chef, the soup chef, the fish chef and the pastry chef, and they each prepare their various ingredients. Then it all comes to the head chef who has to cook it and season it, making sure that all the ingredients work together as an entire meal before he sends it out into the restaurant for people to enjoy. Similarly the mixer takes all the various ingredients that go into making the soundtrack of a movie that each of the specialised sound editors has prepared – dialogue that is recorded on location, dialogue that is added later by the actors, the sound effects and the music – and integrates or mixes these different elements into one carefully prepared whole so when people watch the film nothing sticks out. If during a movie there is suddenly too loud a footstep or a voice goes quieter instead of getting louder you know something is wrong and this pops the suspension of disbelief bubble. It is our job to make it seem as though the way you hear it is the way it always was. In reality it is all very highly manipulated. Everything that you hear has been chosen, fussed over and placed there purposefully. Few people realise that the soundtrack is as manipulated as the picture, and in some cases even more so. Most people will think that it is the way that it always was and that maybe we just added music. That's good because we work very hard to make sure that nobody knows what we're doing.

The mixer will normally start by balancing the dialogue tracks. The dialogue that is recorded on location represents the most immediate and intense expression of the actor's craft. There is an intensity and a directness that comes from knowing that the cameras are rolling and that people are spending hundreds of thousands of dollars a day just to get your performance. In terms of conveying emotion, actors rely very heavily on their voice, so capturing the voice and maintaining the actor's nuances is one of the main jobs of dialogue mixing. Generally there may be a lot of extraneous noises and bangs on the recorded dialogue. All this junk around the actor's performance has to be stripped away leaving you with the essence of their performance as expressed in their voice. A scene may be made up with many

shots of several different people talking. Each shot may come from a different take and a different angle. Each of these takes and angles will sound slightly different but the mixer must balance them to all sound the same without the volume jumping around as though you were in the room. On an average feature of 90 minutes maybe a week is spent just preparing the dialogue so that it sounds smooth and right to the audience. At the same time it does surprise me how little the audience notices. Before the preview screening of Bruce Lee's **Enter the Dragon** we were missing a line that was very important for the plot. Bruce Lee is in his office typing and this character comes in who should say "There's a film that we want you to do, it's called **Enter the Dragon**." Well the actor on the shoot had said "There's a film we want you to do", but he never said, "it's called **Enter The Dragon**". We got this guy who was working with us to record the line just for the preview. It was obviously a completely different person because you hear "There's a movie we want you to do" and then this entirely different voice says, "it's called **Enter the Dragon**". Then it goes back to the original actor saying, "Can you do it?". It was so bad that we in the sound crew did not want it there but it was such an important point in the story that there was really no choice. After the preview I went out into the lobby and started talking to people asking them "Well what did you think of the soundtrack?" Normally they replied "Oh the music was great, I loved it." Then I would quiz them specifically about the scene with the added line. "Do you remember anything unusual about that scene?" They paused. "No." "Was there anything unusual about that particular line?" "No." So even being extremely specific with everybody

The pitch of Matthew Modine's voice in **Equinox** (3) was changed in the mix. In the film he played a bad twin (who was given a low pitch) and a good twin (who was given a high pitch). In **The Talented Mr Ripley** (1–2) Matt Damon had to convincingly mimic the voice of Jude Law's father. The sound editors were able to inter-cut syllables from Damon's lines with the father's so that you could not tell who was talking. "Technically it worked, but the human ear is so exquisitely sensitive to continuity and voice quality that we ended up using Damon's own impersonation." The mixer has to blend in the music with the dialogue and effects in a way that integrates it with the image and the story. "For **The Talented Mr Ripley** composer Gabriel Yared wrote musical themes driven by the story. For example, there is a mischief theme used when Ripley is engaged in lying or devious behaviour. So when he starts to have a relationship with Meredith to further his own ends we hear the mischief theme, but re-scored with soprano sax and strings to give it a romantic theme."

1

2

"The music in **Amadeus** (1–3) is unique because it is a major character like Salieri and Mozart. These three main 'characters' are in the scene where Mozart is writing his last requiem and Salieri is helping him (3). As they talk you hear the music."

3

I asked, nobody was aware that it was a completely different person. So on the one hand we work and make sure that everything is perfect and that the voice quality matches so that the most discerning ear can't tell the slightest bit of difference. And on the other hand people wouldn't recognise it if a truck came through the scenery! In any case there is a lot of pride in craftsmanship. Indeed mixing is a very interesting combination of engineering, craftsmanship, art and creativity: you are called upon to know the technical aspects of what you are doing, produce a finely crafted work, and at the same time be creative in terms of solving problems and situations.

The background sound effects that you hear during a scene (like the city roar or the crickets at night) and the loudness (or level) at which they are mixed in creates a sort of sonic space within which all the other action happens. If you go from a loud party with lots of people talking into a quiet bedroom then you know by the contrast that you are far away even though you are in the same house. If the bedroom is still noisy but not quite as much then you know that you are close to where the main action of the party is. The sound also tells you something about the construction of the house in terms of the thickness of the doors, or if there are drapes in the room. A lot of subtle spatial cues are given by the sound in the same way that the porpoise explores its world by bouncing sounds off things. We get a very immediate although unconscious sense of space and location and material just from the way things sound. So the mixer is creating a world which differs depending on how he mixes together the sounds.

There are two very different kinds of movies and this relates directly to how loud I mix in effects. There are the dramatic films that make use of classical dramatic devices of plot and character, conflict and resolution. These films don't necessarily depend on sound effects to influence the viewer. An effect that is three times louder is not necessarily three times better because the energy and excitement comes from an internal motivation – depending on the degree to which you identify with the characters. Then there is the other class of films, the so-called "ride" films, which rely for their excitement and their energy on external stimulus. They are like going on a roller-coaster where the thrill is being jerked around and having your stomach in your throat in anticipation of going over the hump. In this case external forces generate most of the excitement. Therefore the louder the effects, the heavier the bass, and the more shrieking the music, the more exciting the film is. So effects played three times louder are three times better and it is more exciting. Both of these kinds of films use the same medium for exhibition – they both take place in movie theatres – but they are really two very different beasts. So you have to approach the sound and the attitude of how you deal with these two kinds of films completely differently. Lastly the mixer will add in the music. For me music defines the emotional space of a scene or film in a similar way that the sound effects or the backgrounds will define the physical space. A proper musical score can also enhance the identity of individual characters who have a musical theme that changes as the character undergoes transformations during the film. My role as a mixer is to make the music sound as good as possible. I must be sensitive, both

3

4

5

If music and sound effects are not working together in a scene "it is like two people trying to be in the same place at the same time – it's basically a train wreck!" The mixer will experiment and see which works best. The use of music (Wagner's *Ride of the Valkyries*) when the village is attacked in **Apocalypse Now** (3–5) was extremely well integrated within the scene, starting as "source" music from one of the helicopter speakers. This music had been conceived in the script, the scene was shot with it in mind and the editor spent months cutting the sequence leaving room for both the music and sound effects. The complete mix for **Apocalypse Now** took nine months. Sometimes either sound effects or music will dominate. Maurice Jarre had written a complete musical score for **The Mosquito Coast** (1–2). At the mix when they came to the scene where the ice-making machine in the jungle comes to life, director Peter Weir decided to try dropping the musical score and only hear the sound effects of creaking and hissing. Once the idea was planted, he continued to drop the music throughout the mix. "In the end, apart from the credits, only one piece of the whole score remained in the final film!"

editing & post-production

1

2

3

In **The Right Stuff** (1–3) a sound effect is used to identify the press corps who appear throughout the film (3). In the book author Tom Wolfe had compared them to a hoard of chittering locusts that descend upon a scene and devour every scrap of information in sight. So the sound editors created a chittering insect sound mixed with the sound of cameras whirring and flash bulbs popping. Every time you see the press corps you hear this sound. There is always sound on the track.

4

5

6

In **The English Patient** the problem was creating silence in the desert (6–7). One of the solutions was to start with something (a light wind or small bug) and then take it away. Then you are left with silence. "The art and craft is that people don't notice. One of the most effective ways of creating excitement and tension is by contrast. In **The Unbearable Lightness of Being** (4–5) the first inkling of the Russian invasion of Prague is not the loud tanks but the high pitched rattling of crockery and cutlery. Only then do we cut to the heavy low-pitched rumbling of the tanks. In deciding how loud to play a certain sound I am guided by William Blake in 'The Marriage of Heaven and Hell' – 'you never know how much is enough until you have too much'. I just keep adding until I feel there is too much!"

7

The mixer creates a soundscape that matches the film. In **One Flew Over the Cuckoo's Nest** (2) the windows of the ward are always sealed isolating it from the world. This had a direct impact on what sounds can be heard in the soundtrack. What is heard does not have to be realistic. One scene in **Amadeus** (1) features Mozart walking through a noisy street before going upstairs to his apartment where the window is open. The sound editors continued the street sounds throughout the apartment scene but these sounds were dropped in the mix. "The director said that was the street and that he was only interested in the characters. Another director might have wanted to constantly maintain a sense of the city through the use of sound. It is a matter of taste."

to the emotional nature of what is going on on the screen and the emotional content of the music, making sure that they complement each other. I must also be aware if a musical cue is helping or hindering a scene and how it relates to all the other music in the film. Unfortunately movies are often now being used as kind of sonic billboards for audio product placement. A studio will own a particular track or band and the job of the music supervisor will be to find as many places in the film where they can stick in this music so they can sell records. So a scene in a restaurant or in an automobile becomes like a blank billboard because you can put down a track over the "muzak" in a restaurant or on the car radio. Sometimes it's handled very well where the music is related to the score. Other times it is just to sell records. As the studios become more involved in the music industry films are used more as advertising devices rather than having a music score or a track that is actually needed.

Mixing all this together involves moving faders. But this technical engineering part of the mix is only 20 per cent of what I do. 50 to 60 per cent is ambiance management; maintaining the flow of ideas and making sure everyone feels free to make suggestions. The mixer should try to make it an enjoyable process for people so that they don't get bound up in battling egos with the music department and the effects department coming to blows (which has almost happened several times). The mixer often also has to deal with what I call "separation anxiety". This is particularly common among first-time directors but I've seen it strike more established directors too! As it comes near the end of the mix the director cannot let go. He or she is always looking for things to change. You must remember that the director has been working on this film for at least a year, sometimes maybe two or three years. During this period it has consumed his or her entire life. Suddenly the director will revisit and try to change things that you have gone over a dozen times and were settled with everybody happy. Sometimes it takes a producer coming in and saying "Right, that's it, you've got to finish!" Because all of this process that started with the script, went through the shoot and months of post-production, has all got to end at the mix. It is now time for the public to view the film. When people first become aware of the post-production process and what is going on in a soundtrack you start to think dialogue, music, effects, foley and this cut and that cut. It can all be very disturbing. At first it totally pops the bubble. But after a while when you integrate it into the experience, you will have a much more satisfying and fuller understanding of what is going on and what the post-production crew were doing. It is like learning about a Mozart symphony or a Bach cantata – you begin to hear all the voices and you become aware of the rhythm and how it has been constructed. At the same time you are able to experience the whole thing. Likewise by being able to shift your focus from experiencing a film as one piece to being aware of individual sounds and cuts enhances your appreciation of a movie overall. So at first it will ruin and destroy your appreciation and you will never look at films the same way again, but that is sort of the point – to give you a different way of looking at film. I think it increases your enjoyment and it makes you more aware of the richness of a well-made film.

glossary

ADR (Automatic Dialogue Replacement): The replacement of dialogue in post-production by an actor who repeats lines in sync with the original recording while watching a projection of the original picture (also known as **Looping**).

Assembly: The first stage in cutting after synchronising the rushes. Usually selected takes joined together in script order.

Atmosphere: Sound effect of a general background noise such as restaurant chatter, birdsong, city centre noise etc.

AVID: Trademark of a type of computer non-linear editing system.

CGI (Computer Generated Imagery): A piece of film containing a visual effect created digitally in a computer. Very sophisticated image manipulation can be created by CGI.

Conforming: Process of cutting master or original negative to match the cutting copy or work print in preparation for printing.

Dailies: Unedited picture and sound material from the previous day's shoot which is made ready for synchronisation, normally screened for the crew (also known as **Rushes**).

Dialogue: Speech delivered by the actors in any one scene, either recorded during the original performance or replaced through **ADR** at a later stage.

Digitise: The act of putting footage from tapes (which have been **Telecined**) on to a computer hard drive where they can be stored and then cut. The picture and sound is then in a digital format.

Dissolve: An optical effect where the outgoing shot is faded out while the incoming shot is faded in. More than one shot can be faded in or out at any one time.

Dolly: A platform with wheels on which the camera is mounted to allow smooth movement.

Dub: The process whereby all the tracks of sound (**Foley, ADR, Atmospheres, Dialogue,** music) are mixed together into the single track the audience hears on the final film (also known as the **Mix**).

Fade: An **Optical** effect which involves the picture fading down to black (fade-out) or fading up from black (fade-up). Could also be a colour rather than black.

Feet: Film is measured in feet and frames. Every foot is made up of 16 frames.

Foley: Recording in post-production of sounds made by human movement such as footsteps and clothes rustling. This is done by specialised foley artists re-enacting the sounds in sync while watching a playback of the picture.

Footage: The measurement of film, measured in **Feet**. Also the accumulated material for a film.

Frame: Film is made up of individual pictures or frames which, when projected in sequence, give the illusion of movement. Film is projected at 24 frames per second.

Freeze-frame: An optical effect where one frame is held for a particular length of time through the repeated printing of that frame.

Grading: The process whereby the colours of the final print are checked and modified in the laboratory so that all the shots in a scene match. This is done once the film has been completed (also known as **Timing**).

Horse: The device on an editing bench that is designed for mounting rolls of film by the insertion of rods through apertures in vertical sections. Especially valuable when working with many short sections of film.

Jump-cut: The "jump" effect created by removing a section from the middle of a shot and joining the remaining head and tail of the shot.

Key numbers: Numbers that run alongside the edge of film stock and are visible on the negative when developed. They provide a co-ordinating reference for matching. By looking at the numbers on the cut rush print, the negative can be matched exactly to the cutting copy.

Lightworks: Trademark of a type of computer non-linear editing system.

Looping: (see **ADR**).

Magnetic track (or Mag): The film on which the sound is carried and then cut in a film cutting room.

Mix: (see **Dub**).

Moviola: Trademark for an upright machine used to view film.

Negative: This is the raw footage which comes out of the camera. It needs to be processed at a laboratory before a print can be struck from it. Negative is the original film and therefore very valuable. It is only cut once at the **Negative cutting** stage.

Negative cutting: The process of cutting the original **Negative** to match the cut which the editor has made on computer or rush print.

Negative cutter: The person who cuts the original **Negative** to match the final cut of the film as made by the editor.

Non-linear editing: Editing carried out on computer which facilitates digital storage and random access.

Optical effects (or opticals): A piece of film with an effect such as a **Wipe**, **Dissolve**, or **Fade**.

Pick-up shot: An additional shot taken of a section in a scene which it is felt has been inadequately covered by the other shots. It is taken either at the end of the shooting for a particular scene or after the material has been processed and viewed.

Reel: A feature film, due to the physical bulk of film, is divided up into reels of between 1000 and 2000 feet or 11 and 22 minutes. The projectionist knows one reel is coming to an end and to start the next reel by the appearance of marks in the top right-hand corner of the frame.

Rushes: (see **Dailies**).

Scene: The script is divided up into various scenes or dramatic events unified by time and location.

Set-up: (see **Slate**).

Skip print: When a film is printed every other frame.

Slate: Any scene will be filmed with a number of planned shots each with a particular lighting "set-up" and camera position and each known as a **Slate** or **Set-up**.

Spool: A reel for holding wound-up film, either solid or of the split variety.

Steenbeck: Trademark of a flat-bed (like a table) editing machine used to view and cut film.

Synchronise: The act of matching the picture with the correct sound. Picture and sound are recorded separately on the shoot and arrive separately in the cutting room.

Take: When a director shoots a certain **Set-up** or **Slate** he will continue to shoot it until he gets it right. Each time he shoots it is termed a take.

Telecine: The machine for transferring image from film on to videotape.

Timing: (see **Grading**).

Trim: A piece (or pieces) of film left over when the editor cuts out a bit of film to use in a cut.

Trim bin: The device in which trims are hung or clipped while the material for a sequence is being cut. It should be cleared constantly during editing and the trims re-filed to avoid the problem of not having immediate access to any piece of film.

Voice-over (or VO): Lines that you do not see being delivered on screen, often a narration.

Wipe: An optical effect in the form of a hard-edged line which travels across the screen simultaneously removing the outgoing shot while revealing the incoming one.

picture credits

Courtesy of The Ronald Grant Archive: p 2 Photograph of Jean-Luc Godard; p 12 **Ben-Hur**, MGM; p 16 **Seven Brides for Seven Brothers**, MGM (1, 2); p 18 **The Front Page**, Universal (4); p 20 **Ben-Hur**, MGM (2–4); p 21 **Ben-Hur**, MGM (6); p 22 **The Thomas Crown Affair**, United Artists (1); p 24 **Hana-Bi**, Bandal Visual; p 27 **Hana-Bi**, Bandal Visual (17–19); p 32 **Seven Samurai**, Toho (1); p 32 **Kagemusha**, Toho/Kurosawa (2); p 33 Photograph of Yasujiro Ozu (15); p 34 **Brother**, Recorded Picture/Office Kitano (2–4); p 42 **The Godfather**, Paramount (1); p 44 Photograph of D.W. Griffith (2); p 52 **Lawrence of Arabia**, Columbia; p 61 **Out of Sight**, Universal City Studios Production (2, top); p 61 **Out of Sight**, Universal City Studios Production, photograph by Merrick Morton (2, bottom); p 64 **Tirez sur le Pianiste**, Films de la Pleiade; p 67 **Hiroshima, Mon Amour**, Argos/Como/Pathe/Daiei (2, top); p 67 Photograph of Alain Resnais on set (3); p 68 **Les Quatre Cents Coups**, Sedif/Les Films du Carosse/Janus (1); p 68 **A Bout de Souffle**, SNC (3); p 70 **Fahrenheit 451**, Anglo Enterprise/Vineyard (3); p 73 Photograph of Jean-Luc Godard (6); p 74 Photograph of Eric Rohmer (1); p 90 **Three Colours: Blue**, MK2/CED/France 3/CAB/TOR/CANAL +; p 118 **The Hustler**, 20th Century Fox; p 134–135 **JFK**, Warner Bros. (2–4); p 139 **JFK**, Warner Bros. (2); p 144 **William Shakespeare's Romeo & Juliet**, 20th Century Fox; p 147 **Strictly Ballroom**, M&A Film Corp (2); p 148 **Muriel's Wedding**, CIBY 2000 (1–3); p 149 **How to Make an American Quilt**, Universal/Amblin (6); p 156 **Fallen Angels**, Jettone Productions; p 158 **Happy Together**, Block 2 Pictures Inc. (1); p 160 **Happy Together**, Block 2 Pictures Inc. (1, 2); p 161 **Happy Together**, Block 2 Pictures Inc. (4); p 162 **Fallen Angels**, Jettone Productions (1); p 164 **The Silence of the Lambs**, Orion; p 167 **Sleepy Hollow**, Paramount Pictures/Mandalay Pictures (1, 2); p 167 **Cape Fear**, Universal (5, 6); p 168 **Men in Black**, Columbia (1, 2); p 170 **The Silence of the Lambs**, Orion (2); p 171 **Malcolm X**, Warner Bros. (5); p 172–173 **Crouching Tiger, Hidden Dragon**, Columbia/Sony (1–4); p 172 **GoodFellas**, Warner Bros. (13); p 174 **Barton Fink**, Circle Films (3, 4); p 176 **The Right Stuff**, Warner Bros./Ladd Co.; p 179 **The Talented Mr Ripley**, Paramount/Miramax (2); p 179 **Equinox**, SC Entertainment International (3); p 180 **Amadeus**, Orion (1, 2); p 182 **The Mosquito Coast**, Saul Zaentz Company (2); p 183 **Apocalypse Now**, Zoetrope/UA (3–5); p 184 **The Right Stuff**, Warner Bros./Ladd Co. (1, 2); p 185 **The Unbearable Lightness of Being**, Saul Zaentz Company (4, 5); p 185 **The English Patient**, Tiger Moth/Miramax (6, 7).

Courtesy of The Kobal Collection: p 6 **Gladiator**, Dreamworks/Universal; p 15 **High Society**, MGM (1, 2, 4); p 18 **The Front Page**, Universal (1–3); p 20 **Ben-Hur**, MGM (1); p 36 **Apocalypse Now**, Zoetrope/UA; p 41 **Apocalypse Now**, Zoetrope/UA (2, 3); p 42 **The Godfather**, Paramount (2, 3); p 44 Photograph of the Lumière Brothers, courtesy of the Lumière Brothers (1); p 45 Photograph of Edwin S. Porter, courtesy of Edwin S. Porter (5); p 45 Photograph of Sergei Eisenstein, courtesy of Sergei Eisenstein (8); p 46 **The Unbearable Lightness of Being**, Saul Zaentz Company (1, 2); p 48 **The English Patient**, Tiger Moth/Miramax (1); p 54 **Erin Brockovich**, Universal (1); p 56–57 **Lawrence of Arabia**, Columbia (5, 6); p 61 **Out of Sight**, Universal City Studios Production (2, centre); p 62 **The Elephant Man**, Paramount (1, 3, 5, 6); p 76 **Carrie**, United Artists; p 80–81 **Star Wars**, Lucasfilm/20th Century Fox (2, 3, 6); p 86 **The Secret of My Success**, Universal (1); p 88 **High Noon**, Stanley Kramer/United Artists (1); p 93 **One Deadly Summer**, SNC/TF1/CAPAC (2–4); p 94 **Confidential Report/Mr Arkadin**, Sevilla/Mercury Prods (1); p 98 **Three Colours: Red**, MK2/CED/FRANCE 3/CAB/TOR/CANAL + (1); p 102 **Three Colours: Blue**, MK2/CED/FRANCE 3/CAB/TOR/CANAL + (1); p 106 **Charade** (1963) poster, Universal (1); p 109 **The Mission**, Warner Bros. (1–3); p 110–111 **The Killing Fields**, Enigma/Goldcrest (10–13); p 113 **Memphis Belle**, Warner Bros., photography by David Appleby (1, 2); p 113 **The World is Not Enough**, EON Productions (3); p 116 **Twilight**, Paramount (1); p 116 **This Boy's Life**, Warner Bros. (2); p 116 **The Prince and the Showgirl**, Warner Bros. (3); p 123 **America, America**, Warner Bros. (3); p 129 **The Breakfast Club**, Universal (2); p 130 **JFK**, Warner Bros.; p 132 **Good Will Hunting**, Miramax (1), photography by George Kraychyk (2, 3); p 139 **JFK**, Warner Bros. (1, 3); p 140 **Gladiator**, Dreamworks/Universal (1, 4); p 149 **Elizabeth**, Polygram, photography by Alex Bailey (7, 8).

Visual material contributed by Ralph Winters: p 13 Portrait shot; p 23 Picture of Ralph Winters in the cutting room. *Visual material contributed by Yoshinori Ota:* p 25 Portrait shot; p 30–31 Photographs of Yoshinori Ota and assistant at work in the cutting room and relevant paperwork (1–21); p 34 Publicity poster for **Brother** (1), with thanks and acknowledgement to Recorded Picture/Office Kitano. *Visual material contributed by Walter Murch:* p 48 **The English Patient**, notes and comments (2), with thanks and acknowledgement to Tiger Moth/Miramax; p 49 Photographs from **The English Patient** (3), with thanks and acknowledgement to Tiger Moth/Miramax. *Visual material contributed by Anne Coates:* p 53 Portrait shot; p 54 **Erin Brockovich**, photograph of cutting room and notes, and marked up script pages (2–4), with thanks and acknowledgement to Universal. *Visual material contributed by Cécile Decugis:* p 65 Portrait shot. *Visual material contributed by Paul Hirsch:* p 77 Portrait shot; p 87 **Hard Rain**, memo referring to sound mix (5), with thanks and acknowledgement to Mutual Films/Polygram; p 87 **Mighty Joe Young**, notes on near final cut (6), with thanks and acknowledgement to Walt Disney Pictures. *Visual material contributed by Jacques Witta:* p 91 Portrait shot; p 96 **The Double Life of Véronique**, script pages (1), with thanks and acknowledgement to SIDERAL/TOR STUDIOS/CANAL +; p 98–99 **Three Colours: Red**, script pages (1, 5), with thanks and acknowledgement to MK2/CED/FRANCE 3/CAB/TOR/CANAL +; p 101 **Three Colours: Blue**, script page (2), with thanks and acknowledgement to MK2/CED/FRANCE 3/CAB/TOR/CANAL +. *Visual material contributed by Jim Clark:* p 105 Portrait shot, courtesy of Avid Technology; p 110–111 **The Killing Fields**, notes and marked up script pages (1–9), with thanks and acknowledgement to Enigma/Goldcrest; p 113 **The Killing Fields**, notes (4, 5), with thanks and acknowledgement to Enigma/Goldcrest. *Visual material contributed by Dede Allen:* p 119 Portrait shot; p 123 Photograph of Dede Allen in the cutting room (2). *Visual material contributed by Pietro Scalia:* p 131 Portrait shot; p 132 **Good Will Hunting**, script pages (4), with thanks and acknowledgement to Miramax; p 134–135 Slides of the Zapruder film, reference material for **JFK** (1); p 140 **Gladiator** (2), and notes (3), with thanks and acknowledgement to Dreamworks/Universal; p 141 **Gladiator**, memo from Pietro Scalia to Ridley Scott (5), with thanks and acknowledgement to Dreamworks/Universal; p 141 **Gladiator**, computer-generated images of the Colosseum (6), courtesy of Wes Sewell, with thanks and acknowledgement to Dreamworks/Universal; p 142 **Gladiator**, computer-generated images of 360-degree turn around the amphitheatre before the Carthage fight and the tiger fight (7, 8), courtesy of Wes Sewell, with thanks and acknowledgement to Dreamworks/Universal; p 142 **Gladiator**, audience test form (9), with thanks and acknowledgement to Dreamworks/Universal; p 143 Pietro Scalia in the cutting room. *Visual material contributed by Jill Bilcock:* p 145 Portrait shot of Jill Bilcock in cutting room working on **Moulin Rouge**. "MOULIN ROUGE" ™&©2001, Twentieth Century Fox Film Corporation. All rights reserved; p 150 Excerpts from Jill's visual diaries (1–5); p 154 **Moulin Rouge**, production shots (1, 4, 5), with thanks and acknowledgement to "MOULIN ROUGE" ™&©2001, Twentieth Century Fox Film Corporation. All rights reserved. *Visual material contributed by William Chang:* p 157 Portrait shot, with thanks and acknowledgement to Jettone Films Ltd. *Visual material contributed by Skip Lievsay:* p 165 Portrait shot, with thanks and acknowledgement to C5; p 167 **Cape Fear**, track lists (3, 4), with thanks and acknowledgement to C5 and Universal; p 170 **The Silence of the Lambs**, track list (1), with thanks and acknowledgement to C5 and Orion; p 174 **The Barber** (working title), dubbing charts (1, 2), with thanks and acknowledgement to C5; p 174 **Barton Fink**, track list (5), with thanks and acknowledgement to C5 and Circle Films. *Visual material contributed by Mark Berger:* p 177 Portrait shot. *Miscellaneous visual material:* p 17 Mark Sennett editing rooms (5), courtesy Marc Wanamaker Bison Archives; p 17 Robert Flaherty and Helen van Dongen in their makeshift Louisiana cutting room (6), courtesy Museum of Modern Art; p 37 Portrait shot of Walter Murch © Copyright Academy of Motion Picture Arts and Sciences; p 154 **Moulin Rouge** (2), with thanks and acknowledgement to "MOULIN ROUGE" ™&©2001, Twentieth Century Fox Film Corporation. All rights reserved. Photography by Sue Adler (3).

Screengrabs: p 15 **High Society** (3), with thanks and acknowledgement to MGM; p 16 **Seven Brides for Seven Brothers** (3), with thanks and acknowledgement to MGM; p 17 **On the Town** (4), with thanks and acknowledgement to MGM; p 18 **The Front Page** (5), with thanks and acknowledgement to Universal; p 21 **Ben-Hur** (5), with thanks and acknowledgement to MGM; p 22 **The Thomas Crown Affair** (2), with thanks and acknowledgement to United Artists; p 26–27 **Hana-Bi** (1–16), with thanks and acknowledgement to Bandal Visual; p 28 **Hana-Bi** (1–10), with thanks and acknowledgement to Bandal Visual; p 33 **Seven Samurai** (3–8), with thanks and acknowledgement to Toho; p 33 **Kikujiro** (9–14), with thanks and acknowledgement to Sony Pictures Classics; p 38–39 **Apocalypse Now**, with thanks and acknowledgement to Zoetrope/UA; p 41 **Apocalypse Now** (1), with thanks and acknowledgement to Zoetrope/UA; p 44 **The Birth of a Nation** (3), with thanks and acknowledgement to EPIC; p 44 **The Arrival of a Train** (4), with thanks and acknowledgement to the Lumière Brothers; p 45 **The Great Train Robbery** (6), with thanks and acknowledgement to Edison; p 45 **Battleship Potemkin** (7), with thanks and acknowledgement to Goskino; p 46 **The Unbearable Lightness of Being** (3), with thanks and acknowledgement to Saul Zaentz Company; p 50 **The English Patient** (1), with thanks and acknowledgement to Tiger Moth/Miramax; p 56–57 **Lawrence of Arabia** (1–4), with thanks and acknowledgement to Columbia; p 58–59 **Out of Sight**, with thanks and acknowledgement to Universal City Studios Production; p 61 **Above Us the Waves** (1), with thanks and acknowledgement to Rank; p 62 **The Elephant Man** (2, 4), with thanks and acknowledgement to Paramount; p 67 **Night and Fog** (1), with thanks and acknowledgement to Argos/Como; p 67 **Hiroshima, Mon Amour** (2), with thanks and acknowledgement to Argos/Como/Pathe/Daiei; p 68 **A Bout de Souffle** (2), with thanks and acknowledgement to SNC; p 68 **Tirez sur le Pianiste** (4–6), with thanks and acknowledgement to Films de la Pleiade; p 68 **Les Quatre Cents Coups** (7–9), with thanks and acknowledgement to Sedif/Les Films du Carosse/Janus; p 70–71 **Tirez sur le Pianiste** (1, 2, 4), with thanks and acknowledgement to Films de la Pleiade; p 72–73 **A Bout de Souffle** (1–5, 7–13), with thanks and acknowledgement to SNC; p 74 **Ma Nuit chez Maud** (2), with thanks and acknowledgement to Losange; p 78 **Carrie** (1–3), with thanks and acknowledgement to United Artists; p 80–81 **Star Wars** (1, 4, 5), with thanks and acknowledgement to Lucasfilm/20th C Fox; p 83 **The Birds** (1), with thanks and acknowledgement to Universal; p 84 **Notorious** (1–3), with thanks and acknowledgement to RKO; p 86 **The Secret of My Success** (2, 3), with thanks and acknowledgement to Universal; p 87 **Planes, Trains and Automobiles** (4), with thanks and acknowledgement to Paramount; p 88 **Star Wars** (3, 4), with thanks and acknowledgement to Lucasfilm/20th C Fox; p 88 **High Noon** (2), with thanks and acknowledgement to Stanley Kramer/United Artists; p 93 **One Deadly Summer** (1), with thanks and acknowledgement to SNC/TF1/CAPAC; p 94 **Three Colours: Red** (2), with thanks and acknowledgement to MK2/CED/FRANCE 3/CAB/TOR/CANAL +; p 94 **Three Colours: Blue** (3), with thanks and acknowledgement to MK2/CED/FRANCE 3/CAB/TOR/CANAL +; p 95 **The Double Life of Véronique** (4), with thanks and acknowledgement to SIDERAL/TOR STUDIOS/CANAL +; p 96 **The Double Life of Véronique** (2), with thanks and acknowledgement to SIDERAL/TOR STUDIOS/CANAL +; p 98–99 **Three Colours: Red** (3, 4, 6), with thanks and acknowledgement to MK2/CED/FRANCE 3/CAB/TOR/CANAL +; p 101 **Three Colours: Blue** (1), with thanks and acknowledgement to MK2/CED/FRANCE 3/CAB/TOR/CANAL +; p 101 **The Double Life of Véronique** (3), with thanks and acknowledgement to SIDERAL/TOR STUDIOS/CANAL +; p 102 **Three Colours: Blue** (2, 3), with thanks and acknowledgement to MK2/CED/FRANCE 3/CAB/TOR/CANAL +; p 104 **Marathon Man**, with thanks and acknowledgement to Paramount; p 106 **Charade** (2–4), with thanks and acknowledgement to Universal; p 114–115 **Marathon Man** (1–4), with thanks and acknowledgement to Paramount; p 120 **Bonnie and Clyde** (1, 2), with thanks and acknowledgement to Warner Bros.; p 122 **Bonnie and Clyde** (1), with thanks and acknowledgement to Warner Bros.; p 124 **Dog Day Afternoon** (1, 2), with thanks and acknowledgement to Warner Bros.; p 126–127 **Bonnie and Clyde** (1), with thanks and acknowledgement to Warner Bros.; p 129 **The Breakfast Club** (1), with thanks and acknowledgement to Universal; p 136 **JFK** (1–3), with thanks and acknowledgement to Warner Bros.; p 147 **Strictly Ballroom** (1), with thanks and acknowledgement to M&A Film Corp; p 148 **Muriel's Wedding** (4), with thanks and acknowledgement to CIBY 2000; p 149 **How to Make an American Quilt** (5), with thanks and acknowledgement to Universal/Amblin; p 152–153 **William Shakespeare's Romeo & Juliet**, with thanks and acknowledgement to Twentieth Century Fox; p 158 **Happy Together** (2–10), with thanks and acknowledgement to Block 2 Pictures Inc.; p 160–161 **Happy Together** (3, 5), with thanks and acknowledgement to Block 2 Pictures Inc.; p 162 **Fallen Angels** (2, 3), with thanks and acknowledgement to Jettone Productions; p 168 **Men in Black** (3), with thanks and acknowledgement to Columbia; p 170 **The Silence of the Lambs** (3), with thanks and acknowledgement to Orion; p 171 **Malcolm X** (4), with thanks and acknowledgement to Warner Bros.; p 172–173 **GoodFellas** (5–12), with thanks and acknowledgement to Warner Bros.; p 173 **Singin' in the Rain** (14–16), with thanks and acknowledgement to MGM; p 179 **The Talented Mr Ripley** (1), with thanks and acknowledgement to Paramount/Miramax; p 180 **Amadeus** (3), with thanks and acknowledgement to Orion; p 182 **The Mosquito Coast** (1), with thanks and acknowledgement to Saul Zaentz Company; p 184 **The Right Stuff** (3), with thanks and acknowledgement to Warner Bros/Ladd Co.; p 186 **Amadeus** (1), with thanks and acknowledgement to Orion; p 186 **One Flew Over the Cuckoo's Nest** (2), with thanks and acknowledgement to United Artists/Fantasy Films.

index

editing & post-production